Political Obligation
in a
Liberal State

SUNY Series in Political Theory: Contemporary Issues

John G. Gunnell, Editor

Political Obligation
in a
Liberal State

Steven M. DeLue

State University of New York Press

Published by
State University of New York Press, Albany

© 1989 State University of New York

For information, address State University of New York Press,
State University Plaza, Albany, NY 12246

Library of Congress Cataloging-in-Publication Data

DeLue, Steven M., 1945–
    Political obligation in a liberal state / Steven M. DeLue.
        p.   cm.—(SUNY series in political theory.   Contemporary
    issues)
    Bibliography: p.
    Includes index.
    ISBN 0-7914-0092-1.—ISBN 0-7914-0093-X (pbk.)
    1. Political obligation. 2. Liberalism. I. Title. II. Series.
JC329.5.D45   1989
323.6′5′01—dc19   88-39159
                                                                              CIP

10 9 8 7 6 5 4 3 2 1

In honor of my parents,
William and Dorothy DeLue,
and for Karen, Erik, Dan, and Anna DeLue.

Contents

Introduction

My overall concern is to discuss the basis for citizen bonds to the liberal state. Consequently, I start with a basic question: What does it mean for citizens to have a strong as opposed to a weak sense of political obligation to the liberal state? This is an important question because citizens with a weak obligation may be perceived by the state as in the same category as people with no obligation at all. And when citizens have no sense of obligation to the state, they will have no respect for its authority, they may even resent many of its decisions, and they may feel no need to obey the laws or policies they do not accept. The state may then choose to defend itself against people holding a weak obligation by acting with extreme coercion. But in doing so the state threatens its commitment as a liberal regime to promote basic rights and liberties, in order to secure the development of and respect for all persons. Liberal citizens, or citizens committed to support a liberal state, respect the state in part for the fact that it provides basic rights and liberties for the development of persons. If they do, then they do not wish to have the state act illiberally.

The fact that liberal citizens have a commitment to maintain the regime's liberal character raises two problems. If the regime's liberal character is maintained only when citizens have a strong obligation, then what is the *nature* of a strong as opposed to a weak obligation; second, what is the *basis* for people having a strong as opposed to a weak obligation?

The nature of a strong obligation is defined in terms of what it means to have an obligation to the state. A person who has a sense of obligation to authority respects the state's right to make and to enforce general laws and policies. But this does not mean that citizens will always agree with those laws and policies. A person with a strong obligation will, when he disagrees with the state's policies or laws, generally uphold them anyway. Yet it is possible that one will decide to protest the laws one disagrees with. If one does, one chooses civil forms of protest. Here, one protests by showing respect for the state's right to make and to enforce laws. Thus one may work through established legal channels to influence policymakers to change the law. Or one may decide to violate a particular law one disagrees with, but in doing so, one's intent is to "educate" the general public and the policymakers so they will change the laws or policies one dislikes. Throughout, one demonstrates firm support for the constitutional processes of the regime, and thus if one's actions were to encourage general lawlessness, one would stop using disobedience as a protest form. By contrast, a person with a weak obligation chooses noncivil forms of protest. In this case, a person tries to get the state to change a law or a policy by threatening the state's authority. Here, disobedience to particular laws is undertaken with the intent to encourage general disobedience to critical laws, like urging mass refusal to pay taxes, in order to make it difficult for the state to carry out its constitutional duties. The person with a weak obligation says he will desist from this conduct only after the state's policies have been changed.

Turning to the second question, What is the basis for people to have a strong as opposed to a weak obligation? Liberal citizens find desirable the liberal state's commitment to provide basic rights and liberties to secure the development of persons. So, given this fact, why would any liberal citizen have a weak obligation to a state that protected these liberties? The answer to this question derives from the fact that in contemporary liberal society there are two conflicting ways of life. Indeed, the literature on the liberal state, written by both critics and defenders of the liberal regime, reflects a seemingly unresolvable schism existing at the heart of the liberal society. In one view, citizens see society as promoting an individualist view. Here, the state is neutral among competing individually defined ways of life, and the state must support as many diverse ways of life as possible. In the second, communalist way, there is a comprehensive moral doctrine that should inform each person's life, and when citizens live as the doctrine requires they are likely to work together to build a society based on a shared conception of the public good for each of the policy domains of society. To the individualist, the comprehensive moral doctrine is an impediment to freedom, and to the communalist this doctrine is the basis for obtaining dignity. A citizen who advocates one strain may begin to have a weak obligation if the strain he supports is not also fully supported by the state, even when the state supports providing basic rights and liberties for all.

Still, liberal citizens of either strain do share some common values, in addition to respect for rights and liberties, and because of this fact, it becomes possible to discuss the basis for a strong obligation. Liberal citizens seek to be critically reflective persons capable of assessing the worth of social arrangements and then acting effectively upon their assessments in the policy arena. In short, citizens wish to live in a society, governed by a state, whose policies they can justify. But to succeed, it is necessary to give full recognition to the context that makes this goal possible, the cultural setting conducive to an enlarged culture.

In an enlarged culture, citizens understand that a Platonic conception of politics and of political judgment is useless. There is no integrated system of concepts, joined together by a single truth, that can be the basis for determining a collective judgment regarding the many issues that face society. In a Platonic system there is a definitive principle of right, in the case of *The Republic* the ideal of justice, and all judgments about the best way to organize society should embody this principle. All moral contradictions, as they are manifested in different ways of life, are banished in favor of a single way of life deemed morally appropriate for all. But the reality of modern politics is that a thought system of this sort symbolizes a vision of a perfect intellectual order that fails to provide a practical basis for making political judgments. The reason for the failure of a perfectionist form for judgment is that people think and act from diverse understandings of the significance of the major concepts of the political culture, and this fact is necessitated by the individualist-communalist schism.

Liberal citizens know that if they react to this fact of life of liberal society by pushing for a perfectionist view anyway they may undermine the society's commitment to provide rights and liberties to all, and they may also undermine an authentic expression of the strain, individualist or communalist, that they support. Thus to resist divergent views that threaten a truly communalist setting, communalism would be turned into a collectivist form which destroyed the comprehensive moral doctrine on which a search for the common good among the citizens would be based. In this case, the common good would not arise from the citizens and be seen as "their" common good, but the good all were to accept would be viewed as alien to the interests of all citizens. An extreme form of individualism would deny the authentic expression of this strain, too. To promote an extreme form of individualism would sanction a setting that led to a few "super" individuals making others support their way of life, thus denying a chance for an individualist life form to most citizens. In either case, where an extreme form of communalism or individualism is pursued, the basic rights and liberties would be denied to all but the supporters of the triumphant and dominant strain. Needless to say, in both cases, the critically reflective citizen would be seen as dangerous, and thus the critical mentality would have to be denied, too.

Given the view that perfectionist approaches to judgment are a threat to the basic character of a liberal regime, citizens do best when they base judgments pertaining to political issues upon an effort that seeks to narrow the differences among them. The rules that govern this discourse, as well as the central moral sentiment that it is based upon, are of great importance to understanding the nature of the dialog that buttresses liberal society and that permits citizens of diverse views to find a way to accommodate their differences. This book will make, as one of its major objectives, an effort to delineate both the underlying rules of an enlarged discourse and the moral sentiments that sustain it. In undertaking this enterprise, I rely upon two writers in two different enlightenment traditions, Immanuel Kant and Adam Smith.

In doing so, my point is that even in a society with diverse and conflicting views of the best way of life, it is possible to construct a basis for a fruitful public discourse that determines the ends and purposes of public policy, as long as the state can sustain an enlarged relationship to its citizens. If it can, then it has a right to expect from citizens a strong obligation. In this case, the liberal state can continue to maintain its commitment to rights and liberties for all in a manner that citizens see as genuine and justifiable. Moreover, the quest to define the enlarged culture will demonstrate how to turn the central schism in liberal society into a creative force that makes the development of all persons possible.

In consequence, the basis for a strong obligation is that the state provide the conditions that secure an enlarged culture by maintaining an enlarged relationship to citizens. Much of the book, then, is designed to discuss what the state must do in order to achieve this end. In this regard, I discuss the various "signs" of an enlarged citizen-state relationship. Here, I claim, in contrast to those who attack the liberal state by arguing that only participatory democracies create an enlarged culture, that the liberal state with its representative form may manifest an enlarged relationship to citizens if it protects rights in a substantive and not just a formal sense. Rights are granted in a formal sense when through the constitutional process rules for defining rights are determined and then these rules are applied to all citizens. These rights should give citizens the independence needed to challenge openly the state's policies. When the state fully considers the views of all, including the challengers, it secures rights in a substantive sense, too. To accomplish this end, the state must be built upon traditions that enable it to break down corporatist tendencies. In the latter, powerful interests dominate the policy-making process and exclude the rest of the society from consideration in this process. This event threatens the ability of the state to provide rights in a substantive sense and in consequence destroys an enlarged relationship between the state and its citizens. The corporatist dimension is overcome by a strong challenge tradition, which enables citizens to openly question state policies, and by what this tradition helps to produce, a setting of public reason in which public officials resist corporatist interests by maintaining the power of the legislative body to make laws as a result of a fully enlarged discussion of issues. I also discuss as an important sign of an enlarged culture the nature of the social learning process, which teaches that the enlarged discourse is the route to fairness. Finally, I discuss the need and the importance of the society having a political will to provide a material basis for a decent life for all citizens. This is necessary in order to avoid intense social antagonisms which, if allowed to exist, would destroy an enlarged culture.

Finally, in addressing the problems just enumerated in this introduction and throughout the book, it should be clear that I write from the standpoint of what I understand to be the *ideal liberal citizen*. This citizen is concerned to live in a society where the relationship to the state permits all citizens to be critically reflective persons. The foci of their evaluative demeanor are government decisions. Furthermore, the ideal liberal citizen seeks to be politically effective in the effort to make possible a setting that nurtures self-respect and maximum development of all persons. In developing a basis for strong citizen bonds to the state by making clear the central importance of an enlarged culture, the ideal liberal citizen stands for basic practices and traditions that are not in any sense foreign to the liberal project, but which are indeed central to it. I hope, therefore, that the ideal liberal citizen stands for characteristics that are not simply written off as incredulous figments of my imagination. Instead, I hope my view of the ideal liberal citizen is understood as embodying essential characteristics for citizens who are committed to protect the liberal regime from the many elements that threaten it.

I would like to thank those who have directly or indirectly contributed to this book. The idea for this book developed during study on Kant sponsored by the National Endowment for the Humanities. That idea was further developed by the National Endowment for the Humanities summer seminar run by Professor Richard Flathman. Discussions I had with him have been invaluable. Also, I have benefited from the comments on many of my convention papers given at various meetings, including the American Political Science Association, the Midwest Political Science Association, the Southwest Social Science Association, and the Southern Political Science Association. I am most grateful for the thoughtful comments of Professor Richard Dagger. He read the first chapter as a convention paper, and his keen comments helped me to know better what I was trying to say. In particular, his comments helped me to conceptualize the main problem as one of trying to determine the basis for a strong obligation. I would also like to thank Professor Emily Gill for her helpful comments, which resulted in the development of the Adam Smith material. To my good friend Mike Briggs who believed in this project from the beginning and who was a source of constant encouragement, I say thank you. Thanks go too to Peggy Gifford, editor at State University of New York Press, to the anonymous reviewers, and especially to Professor John Gunnell, editor for the SUNY Series in Political Theory: Contemporary Issues, for their thoughtful, helpful, and considerate reading of this book. Thanks go to Sharon Lougheed, Production Editor, for her helpful editing advice and her friendly concern throughout the process. I also remain indebted to my wife, Karen, for her "enlarged understanding" of the many anxieties one encounters with a project of this sort and for her helpful editing. The many shortcomings are still of course mine.

September 1988

1

Political Obligation
in Liberal States

I. INTRODUCTION TO THE MAIN PROBLEM

A. John Simmons concludes a recent book on political obligation by saying that "political theory cannot offer a convincing general account of our political bonds. . . . We must conclude that citizens generally have no special political bonds which require that they obey and support the governments of their countries of residence. Most citizens have neither political obligations nor 'particularized' political duties, and they will continue to be free of such bonds barring changes in political structures and conventions."[1]

Were this attitude to become widely accepted in liberal societies, it would be a tragedy for liberal regimes. To have a political obligation is to respect the state's legal authority to make and to enforce laws and policies. But when citizens have no sense of obligation to the liberal state, citizens will have no respect for its legal authority, they may even resent many of its decisions, and they may feel they have no need to obey the laws they do not accept. In this setting, the state will have no recourse but to maintain itself by force. Certainly all states, including liberal states, rely upon some degree of state coercion to ensure citizen compliance with the state's laws. But where citizens have no sense of obligation to the state's authority, the amount of coercion used may well be excessive.[2]

Moreover, the liberal state that uses excessive coercion in sustaining citizen compliance undermines its character. That character is defined in terms of its commitment to provide basic public rights and liberties to all, as a way to secure a setting that facilitates the develop-

1

ment of and the respect of persons. The basic rights and liberties (discussed in chapter 2) like freedom of speech, thought, conscience, association, private property, and due process of law are what can be called "political liberties." They protect people from the abuses of government authority and thus provide the freedom needed to permit people to have the independence to criticize policies and laws and to work to change them on behalf of their own conceptions of what is best.[3] But when the only basis for citizen obedience is extreme state coercion, the character of the liberal state is radically changed, and its mission to protect basic rights and liberties defeated.

I presume that citizens in a liberal state would wish to avoid excessive coercion because they fear jeopardizing qualities of the liberal state, such as basic rights and liberties, that they find desirable. The loss of independence as a result of the state becoming an instrument for excessive force would not be a condition that most citizens would find acceptable. In taking this view I further presume, then, that citizens in a liberal state, no matter how critical they might be toward its policies, would prefer to maintain the liberal state and its qualities (the protection of basic rights and liberties), and that this preference represents a desire to preserve the liberal character of authority.[4]

Still, it is possible that the desire to maintain the character of a liberal state may by itself only produce a weak obligation to the state, an obligation so weak in fact that in the face of other obligations, political obligations may not be considered primary. When this happens the state may decide that the citizens' orientations to the state have the same impact on the state as if they had no sense of obligation at all. The problem then is that citizens who find the state's qualities desirable may act in ways that are understood to show minimal respect for the state, causing the state to react with excessive coercion. In this case, citizens who support the liberal qualities of the state's character find themselves perceived as acting in a way to threaten those qualities they respect. In the rest of this section, I summarize the reasons that explain why citizens who respect the state's qualities may nonetheless have a weak obligation to the state. I also explain the significance for the state of a weak obligation by contrasting it to a strong obligation.

The liberal state, with its provision of basic rights and liberties, supports different and conflicting conceptions of how life should be lived. (These versions of the way of life will be fully developed in chapter 3.) For some, who hold the individualist view, liberal societies should be designed to facilitate a variety of different, individually defined life-styles. Under this view, citizens wish to choose their own way of life, and the state must remove external constraints that make it impossible for citizens to attain this end. From the individualist point of view, external constraints are permitted only insofar as they enhance the diversity and quality of individual choices for all citizens. For those who hold the communalist view, liberal society should promote communal forms of life in which individuals guide their lives by a set of overarching standards. Here rules and norms, while shaping citizens so that their lives are in tune with a particular moral viewpoint, are welcomed as necessary bonds that save citizens from acting in ways that irreparably harm themselves and others.

Thus citizens will have disagreements with the state over issues of policy, especially when the state takes positions that conflict with the views of the way of life certain citizens may hold. For instance, when called to the army to defend the state's view of the community interest, some citizens may object on the basis of the fact that they hold a different conception of the common good, based on their affiliation with a religious community; or when asked to pay an income tax, certain citizens may object based upon the view that this form of taxation undermines their individualist concept of life; or some religious citizens may find objectionable the state's decision not to permit public school prayer on behalf of the need to protect individual freedom.

In each instance, one can rest one's refusal to obey upon a sense of obligation to a particular view of the best way of life for society, which I will call from this point on "nonstate forms of obligation." What should be clear is that these kinds of conflicts are endemic to liberal societies. Michael Walzer sums up the problem of political obligation well, then, when he says, "the obligations of individual men and women are unlikely to be either singular or stable. We regularly commit ourselves in more than one direction. We convey to different sets of men and women different senses of our own intentions and beliefs; these senses are not necessarily contradictory, nor are they necessarily devoid of contradiction. We also shift the weight of force of our commitments over time."[5]

The question that reflective citizens raise as they assess these conflicts is whether the conflicts symbolize a tendency by the state to move in a direction that threatens if not denies the way of life they most prize. If they conclude that this is the case, then the rights and liberties the state protects lose their significance. Here, even if the state in its official role intensely desires to support the provision of rights and liberties to all, still, citizens for whom these rights lose significance may feel that the state is not really living up to its commitment to provide rights and liberties. In this situation, citizens' sense of political obligation would become weak. This judgment has practical implications for how people relate to authority and for how the state defines its commitment to the liberal character.

Before discussing both how people relate to authority when they have a weak sense of obligation and what the state's reactions to those who hold a weak obligation may be, it is necessary to clarify further what is meant when one has a weak as opposed to a strong obligation to political authority. To have an obligation to political authority is, as I have said, to respect the state's legal authority to make and to enforce general laws and policies. This conception of political obligation, I hasten to add, does not mean that in all cases, citizens will agree with all laws and general policies. In fact, citizens may not agree with particular laws because these laws conflict with nonstate-related views or commitments. When citizens do not agree with particular laws or policies, they must decide how strong their obligation to the state will be. If citizens have a strong obligation, they generally will uphold those laws or policies they disagree with. It should be clear, however, that in a liberal state, citizens may decide to protest the laws or policies they disagree with and still have a strong obligation.

Citizen forms of protest may run from working within established legal channels to change laws or policies to even disobeying a particular law or policy. In the first instance, they may lobby public officials directly and ask them to work to change public policy. In the second instance, citizen protests are designed to convince the public of the importance of the protesters' position in the hope that this enhanced public understanding can successfully pressure public officials to rethink and then to change the policy. Citizens who disagree with a law may decide to make their appeal to the public by acts of civil disobedience. People engaged in civil disobedience violate a particular law to gain from the public a forum for their protest, but in doing so they make sure that the public understands that the target of the protest is only the particular law the civil disobedients want changed. To this end, the protesters make it clear that their protest is not designed to undermine the state's constitutionally established political authority. In either case, whether citizens manifest their disagreement to particular state actions by resorting to legal means or by using civil disobedience, citizens who disagree with a law or policy are said to have a strong obligation to the state because in the course of conducting their protest, they demonstrate respect for the state's right to make and to enforce general laws and policies. These forms of protest are called civil.

In contrast, what characterizes a weak obligation is when citizens who decide to protest a law (either through disobedience or through another tactic), do so in a way that demonstrates minimal respect for the institutions and authority of the government. This form of protest is noncivil. Citizens who have a weak obligation interpret the conflict they have with the state as signifying that on the whole the state does not support the way of life they most prize, and whereas they do have respect for its commitment to rights and liberties, still, they are less concerned (than citizens with a strong obligation) whether the actions they choose in protesting a law will damage the state's authority. Indeed, citizens with a weak obligation to the state have as their first priority the desire to pressure the state into changing policies by threatening its authority. This approach is in contrast to persons who have absolutely no respect for the state's right to make and to enforce laws. These individuals have no sense of political obligation to the state, and they may in fact have as their intention a desire to undermine the state completely. In the case of persons with a weak sense of obligation, however, the tactic to threaten the state's authority is not meant as a statement of an intention to undermine the state's authority. Persons with a weak obligation want the state to remain in place, but with a new set of priorities.

Noncivil protest has several classic forms. In the first type, or what I refer to as pure legal forms, citizens organize a lawful strike in a strategic part of the economy that if carried out is certain from both the citizens' and the state's points of view to bring about economic hardship, and thus make it difficult for the state to secure its ability to govern. If the state wants to keep its authority, it must change its policies or the strike will continue. In another type of noncivil protest, which I call borderline legal, persons with a weak obligation act within the law to use their freedom of speech to convey a message that if carried out would lead many people to act illegally. For instance, because persons do not agree with an offensive weapons buildup, they use their freedom of speech to organize a mass refusal to pay taxes. If that protest is successful, many hundreds of thousands of people may not pay their taxes, thus directly threatening the government's authority. This type of protest straddles the legal and illegal realms because it uses freedom of speech to urge people to refuse to pay taxes and by doing so threatens the state's ability to govern, as a means to get the state to change its policies. In contrast, persons with a strong obligation might refuse to pay taxes as a symbol of their protest to a policy they do not like. Their strategy is to encourage the public to side with them and then to voice their views in the political process in the hope that this public action will cause policymakers to change their views, too. But if their actions led to mass refusal to pay taxes, they would change their mode of protest and choose a form of civil protest which did not threaten the state's authority.

The problem the state faces is that if enough people begin to demonstrate a weak obligation to the state during the course of protesting particular laws, the state may not be able to maintain its authority to make and enforce laws and policies. From the standpoint of a state wishing to protect its authority, it may decide that its only recourse is to treat those manifesting a weak obligation as if they had no obligation at all and were indeed bent upon destroying the state's authority. No doubt this decision would be difficult for the state, because the people the state acts against in this case do in fact have some respect for the state's authority, since even people with a weak obligation share a commitment to maintain basic rights and liberties. Thus, by acting to protect its authority, the state may then be acting against citizens who share the state's commitments. Moreover, in order to act against them, the state may decide that it must, in order to secure its authority against the threats the state confronts, use extreme coercion and act illiberally.[6]

In this case, the state may find ways to override the rights of citizens it decides to act against while giving an appearance of protecting those rights nonetheless. The consequence of this conduct is to diminish, overall, a commitment to protect these rights. For instance, let's say that I am protesting the state's policy on nuclear weapons by refusing to pay my taxes, and further that my hope is to get others to refuse to pay their taxes, too. In this case, I have a weak obligation because I am threatening the state's authority as a means to get it to change its policies. Yet I am not a security risk because I support the state's commitment to protect basic liberties, and I am not desirous of aiding the state's enemies. Still, the state may look upon me as if I were a spy for a foreign power and treat me as a dangerous threat to security by placing me under constant surveillance. It may do so without formally violating my right to privacy because it has acted with court approval under a law that allows it to "watch" security risks. The state may after gathering evidence put me on trial and before and during the trial seek broad publicity for the case, so that the public will think I have probably committed a grave crime. The state may further threaten my rights by dragging out the trial over a long period of time, bringing in mountains of questionable evidence against me. As a result, I lose my job and I have to shoulder huge legal costs to defend myself. The trial accords me all my basic rights under the due process requirements, but because I do not have the financial means to defend myself adequately, I am convicted, and the judge, again acting within the law and by request of the state, which wants to make an example of me, sentences me to a severe prison sentence. The state's extreme action, even if undertaken in a way to make it appear as if it protects my liberties, ends up undermining them both for me and for others. My rights are compromised because, owing to the circumstances of my trial, I am denied a chance to use them effectively. Others' rights are undermined because others might hesitate to use the rights which permit them to protest state actions owing to the fear that similar forms of repression would be used against them, too.

This is not the state's reaction when it has conflicts with citizens who demonstrate a strong sense of obligation, because people with a strong obligation do not protest policies they disagree with by threatening the state's authority. The liberal state, committed as it is to sustain basic rights and liberties for all, does best for this objective, then, when it can maintain among its citizens a strong sense of obligation.

The issue of political obligation emerges as critical precisely at this point. Liberal citizens not wanting to see the demise of those aspects of liberal states they find desirable, the protection of basic rights and liberties for all, realize that only a strong sense of obligation will prevent this outcome. But to maintain such a strong sense of obligation, citizens expect that the state must act in such a way as to justify a strong obligation, and the problem here is that the state's protection of rights and liberties will not by itself provide that justification. Therefore, to justify a strong obligation to a liberal state, additional grounds must be provided.

The justification for a strong obligation must, as I argue in chapter 3, demonstrate to holders of either an individualist or communalist view a basis for sustaining a strong obligation to authority even when they disagree with particular positions taken by the state. Political philosophy has the job of demonstrating when it is necessary for citizens to assert in the face of nonstate demands a strong obligation to the state, one that justifies continued respect for the state's right to make and to enforce laws, even as they may conclude that the state's decisions on particular questions pertaining to nonstate relationships are mistaken.

II. THE BENEFITS RECEIVED VIEW

In this section, I discuss the benefits received view of political obligation, based on Rawls's fairness principle, and in the next section I discuss the shortcomings of Rawls's argument that political bonds should be based not on a notion of obligation but on a notion of a natural duty of justice. The discussion of Rawls in the next section adds support to my general claim that the particular version of the benefits received view argued for in this section provides the best approach to demonstrating the basis for a strong political obligation to a liberal state.

Rawls's principle of fairness holds that people who benefit from a mutually cooperative and *just* social arrangement should adhere to the rules of the social arrangement they benefit from, and further that they have a right to expect that others who benefit from such a social arrangement should uphold the rules of the scheme, too.[7] Thus, for Rawls the fairness principle presumes that obligations arise when an "institution is just (or fair), that is, it satisfies the two principles of justice [described in footnote 1, chapter 7]; and second, one has voluntarily accepted the benefits of the arrangement or taken advantage of the opportunities it offers to further one's interests."[8] Obligations arise within a mutually advantageous and just cooperative setting where persons voluntarily enter into arrangements whose requirements they agree to accept in exchange for the benefits they expect to receive. Further, in indicating their acceptance of these benefits, persons make clear their understanding that the scheme they freely enter is a cooperative setting that produces the benefits they desire and that to continue to gain benefits from this setting, it is only "fair" that they, as well as other members, contribute to it in the manner required to maintain it.

It should be noted, however, that Rawls does not make the fairness principle the basis for establishing a general citizen obligation to political authority, for as we see in the next section, he bases citizen bonds on a duty to act justly. Instead, Rawls predicates a host of other obligations on the fairness principle, including those associated with political officeholders and many other nonpolitical kinds of association like marriage or game participation where there is an "obligation to play by the rules and be a good sport."[9] But others who see virtue in the benefits received view do indeed seek to make this principle the foundation of a general obligation to political authority. Thus, for George Klosko, "the principle of fairness can be used most plausibly to establish political obligations by appealing to society's provision of important public goods."[10] Furthermore, one may become obligated to abide by the laws of a political regime one benefits from even if one has not "accepted" the benefits, as Rawls's view of obligation based on the principle of fairness would require, and even if one is unaware "of the status of the benefits as products of cooperative scheme."[11] Klosko says that "as long as the benefits in question are sufficiently large, someone 'who is simply going about his business in normal fashion' benefits unavoidably from a cooperative scheme does indeed incur an obligation to contribute to the scheme."[12]

Klosko's approach has merit for the reason that it emphasizes that states, which are mutually cooperative schemes, must provide "sufficiently large" public benefits if people are to have a political obligation to them. Klosko avoids predicating political obligations simply on the notion that people should be bound to uphold the requirements of mutually cooperative and fair schemes they benefit from, whether they have agreed to accept the benefits of the arrangement or whether they understand themselves to be taking advantage of its opportunities. This last view is an approach that has the liability of justifying bonds to nonstate associations that may be in the end stronger than obligations to the state. For citizens are members of many mutually cooperative nonstate associations, and citizens may benefit from each type in the normal course of their lives. Moreover, it is possible that citizens may conclude that they benefit more from nonstate associations than from their relationship to the state. This is a problem when the requirements of each type of association conflict.

When the two types of obligations come into conflict, one must determine which one is stronger. Of course, citizens who go through life benefiting from cooperative schemes, it is true, may never be forced to confront these questions if no conflicts emerge between the state and nonstate associations. But a conflictless world is only possible within a hyperideal vision, and this possibility is not the way of life found in ordinary experience. As a consequence, people have to determine if they will have a stronger obligation to the state than to a nonstate association. Klosko's approach has merit, then, because in arguing that political obligations should arise from a cooperative scheme providing major benefits, one has a basis for resolving this conflict and establishing a strong obligation to the state. This is the thrust of the argument here, and in the example that follows, a particular conflict is detailed in order to demonstrate why it is important to determine the nature of essential state benefits as the basis for resolving the conflict.

Let's say in the day-to-day course of my life I use the relatively inexpensive electricity from a state-licenced nuclear power plant.[13] But I do not like the plant because I think it is a danger to health and to the environment. I accept that society is on the whole a fair scheme that provides benefits I like, as in this case cheap electricity, which I need and use, and thus on the logic of the benefits received view, I should pay the taxes requested of me by the state even if it has used its authority to licence the plant. But let's also assume I am a member of a group protesting these plants. This group is also (for its members) a mutually advantageous cooperative arrangement, and it works to provide to all citizens who wish to join a chance to participate in politics effectively; in this case, for the purpose of eliminating nuclear power plants. The problem is that the group has decided to protest the plant by urging the state to withdraw the plant's licence to operate. At first, the group resorts to an effort to educate the relevant state officials on the issue, hoping that the effort will convince them to withdraw the licence. But this tactic does not succeed. So after experiencing this failure, the antinuclear group decides that its only recourse is to organize a massive tax refusal campaign. At this point, two conflicting obligations exist for me, and the question is which one should be given higher priority. If I have a strong obligation to the state, either I will pay the taxes or I will protest through means that show respect for the state's authority. In the latter case, if I decide not to pay taxes, I will do so only if I can be certain that my action will be seen as a form of education that will culminate in the public deciding to bring pressure on the state to make it withdraw the licence. But I will not use this tactic if I think it will encourage many others to refuse to pay their taxes, too. If I have a weak obligation to the state, I will protest the state's policy on nuclear power by threatening its authority and refusing to pay taxes, hoping even to ignite a general taxpayers' revolt in which many thousands of people refuse to pay.

In this situation, if one can determine the major benefits that governments must provide, as is the thrust of Klosko's work, then one can say that when the government provides them, there is certainly a basis for justifying a strong obligation to the state. To determine the major benefits a state should provide, it is necessary to indicate for a particular regime what citizens generally value, and once this has been done, then one must demonstrate what conditions contribute most to these values. In the case of the liberal state, citizens value basic rights and liberties and citizens hold the hope that these rights and liberties can be used to contribute to the development of persons. In particular, liberal citizens, as stated earlier and as argued more extensively in chapter 3, value two different views of how the development of persons can be realized, individualist and communalist. Further, as I argue in chapter 3 as well, it becomes clear to liberal citizens that both forms of life must be understood as necessarily copresent in society. This is the case even if the two views tend to conflict with each other. Nonetheless, it becomes clear to liberal citizens that neither view can maintain essential aspects of itself unless it can exist in a society which contains the other view as well. As a result, what helps to sustain this tension in a manner useful to each view helps to maintain a setting in which the rights and liberties are provided in a manner respectful of both ways of life. Here the essential benefits of a liberal society are the conditions it creates to make possible a setting of this sort.

If the liberal state provides these benefits, then there is evidence to justify a form of de facto consent.[14] The term *consent* is not meant to indicate a form of expressed consent or a deliberate decision to abide by the state that provides these benefits, but instead the basis for saying citizens have consented is that the state has provided benefits so essential to sustaining basic liberal values that no liberal citizen who shares these values could argue against having a strong obligation to the state without appearing unreasonable or lacking in common sense. In this case, then, people who gain essential benefits from a political regime can say not only that the regime is a mutually cooperative, beneficial scheme, but that it is one worthy of a strong obligation.

This is an important point because at issue in any discussion of political obligation is the problem of whether citizens can be said to voluntarily accept the regime's authority. As Rawls points out, an obligation presumes voluntary acceptance of certain requirements in exchange for perceived benefits. But citizens neither have a chance to formally consent to the constitution of their regime nor in most instances do they formally and directly even consent to particular laws. still, the act of consent is manifested by the way citizens respond to state policies they disagree with. Citizens who disagree with state policies but who as a consequence of the state's provision of essential benefits manifest a strong as opposed to a weak sense of obligation to the regime, demonstrate a type of informal consent to the regime. In choosing to have a strong sense of obligation to the regime, citizens demonstrate indirectly a desire to consent to the regime, and the reason for this decision is that it would not be in any reasonable person's interest to threaten a regime which secures things that they value highly and that they need in order to achieve their greatest hopes.

For Rawls, as we see in the next section, this kind of argument, because it is not based on formal and direct consent, fails to provide a basis for citizen bonds to the state. Thus he suggests basing political bonds on a natural duty of justice. I suggest, however, that his argument for a duty to obey a just regime raises the same problems that

I confronted in the discussion of how to determine a strong obligation, and thus the most important question is once again the nature of the essential benefits a state must provide to secure from citizens support in a strong sense.

III. RAWLS AND A DUTY OF JUSTICE

For Rawls, as just indicated, the "basing of political ties upon a princi- ple of obligation would complicate the assurance problem."[15] To do so requires that a citizen's political obligation be based on consent to a just or fair scheme, and then one must make citizen bonds "in some appropriate sense voluntary," but Rawls says it is difficult to find a "plausible account" of a voluntary commitment. If one insists on con- sent as the basis for citizen bonds, "the public conviction that all are tied to just arrangements would be less firm, and a greater reliance on the coercive powers of the sovereign might be necessary to achieve stability. But there is no reason to run these risks."[16] So Rawls bases political bonds on a "natural duty to comply with the constitution [of a just state]," and a "just state" is defined in terms of his principles of justice (see footnote 1, chapter 7).[17] Thus, unlike a political obligation which suggests voluntary compliance with citizen bonds, a political duty suggests that compliance is based on a categorical command to live by and to be bound by morally justified rules.

But the approach Rawls suggests has its own difficulties, and these problems stem from the fact that a natural duty is understood in a broad sense by Rawls. For instance, citizens have various natural duties including the duty to help another when in need or jeopardy, provided that one can do so without excessive risk to oneself,[18] and the duty of mutual respect, which is one of the most important natural duties.[19] This duty requires one to view situations from other persons' perspectives and give reasons for one's actions "whenever the inter- ests of others are affected."[20] All presumably benefit when people manifest mutual respect, and it is the mark of a moral personality to do so; in fact a moral person is willing at times to sacrifice his self- interest to sustain mutual respect.[21]

Another important natural duty is the duty of justice, which requires "us to support and to comply with just institutions that exist and apply to us." For Rawls a natural duty of justice binds people generally, it is more fundamental than an obligation, "and [it] requires no voluntary act in order to apply."[22] But this general bond, as herein defined, does not itself explain how conflicts between duties are to be handled, nor does it demonstrate on what basis a duty to the state is stronger than a nonstate duty. When the two types of duties come into conflict, how is the conflict to be resolved? On what basis is one duty, say the duty to aid others in need, made consistent with the duty to obey the law of a just state, when rendering aid may require a person to break the law?

This kind of problem is faced, for instance, when citizens from a sense of the need to aid others give sanctuary to illegal aliens who would lose their lives if forced to return to their countries of origin. In giving sanctuary, citizens demonstrate their desire to maintain a duty to help others and to protest an alien return law, which they find morally objectionable. They choose to protest this law by direct and public disobedience. The state, in deciding to prosecute people for their disobedience, may argue that these citizens are not upholding their duties to the state, which should take first priority over other duties these citizens say they have. In fact, the state's decision may indicate that when citizens give sanctuary as a form of protest, their actions may well manifest a threat to the state's authority. Thus, the state could argue that this form of protest actually harms the state's ability to control its population increases from external sources and by doing so threatens the state's ability to maintain control over one of its most essential concerns. The state might say that citizens have every right to protest a law they find morally objectionable, but citizens should find ways of protesting that do not impair its authority.

But citizens would then demand a reason for placing a higher priority on duty to the state so that they would relate to the state in a way that manifested a strong sense of duty to it and which, like a strong obligation to the state, would allow citizens to be justified in not pursuing a form of protest (to laws they disagreed with) that threatened the state's authority. In response, Rawls would argue that if the state is just by virtue of providing basic rights and liberties, then citizens should have a strong duty to uphold its authority. But in actuality, those who from conscience feel a natural duty to aid others may say that the state is really not acting in keeping with its commitment to basic rights and liberties when it does not allow certain people, who may suffer death if returned to their home country, to remain in this country. Here, the claim is made that providing basic rights and liberties means that the state must respect the right of conscience by permitting citizens to act as their conscience dictates and extend aid to others. But in not doing so, the state acts against its own principles. For citizens to accept a state decision of this type and to pursue a form of protest which does not threaten its authority, citizens would expect additional, more compelling arguments. (This question is the subject of chapter 4.)

Of course, Rawls does claim that in trying to balance duties that conflict with each other or with obligations, "there are no obvious rules for settling these questions."[23] And his intent in developing, for instance, his account of civil disobedience is to begin to provide an explanation of how to address this conflict.[24] But clearly, throughout, his tendency is to emphasize a higher, more compelling duty to uphold the laws of a just state, where justice is defined as the state's provision of basic liberties. Thus, civil disobedience is generally restricted both to violations of the principle of equal liberty, or the principle of providing the same rights and liberties to all, and to "blatant" violations of the principle of fair equality of opportunity, or the notion that economic inequalities should be arranged so that they are "attached to positions and offices open to all." In contrast, infractions of the difference principle, and here Rawls means the requirement to arrange social and economic equalities so that they are to everyone's advantage, involve a wide range of opinions. These matters may invoke self-interest concerns among citizens, and thus unless a particular distribution threatens a basic liberty, the laws upholding that distribution should not be protested by civil disobedience.[25] This view contains the notion that there is a bias in favor of resolving conflicts between duties by requiring citizens to uphold the requirements of a state that protects basic liberties. But even a state committed to protect basic liberties may support a law that appears to threaten a particular liberty for some people without intending to undermine the overall commitment to secure basic rights and liberties for all. In this case, should citizens who elect to protest such a law show a strong duty to the state by using, as people do when they manifest a strong obligation, civil means? That a state intends to secure basic liberties or that there is a duty of justice to adhere to the laws of such a state are factors which by themselves fail to answer this question.

Once again the problem of why one should have a strong bond to the state is left unsolved. If this is so, then the question of which view is best in justifying citizen bonds, duty or obligation, appears semantical and diminishes in favor of determining what major benefits the state should provide that would evoke a strong sense of respect for the state, leading citizens to have either a strong obligation or strong duty to uphold the state's laws.

IV. GRATITUDE AND POLITICAL OBLIGATION

Before discussing the full nature of the essential benefit that creates a basis for a strong obligation, it should be clear why the basis for a political obligation cannot be an obligation of gratitude. I make this claim by first discussing what gratitude as a basis for political obligation signifies, and then I demonstrate why gratitude is an inadequate basis for founding a political obligation to authority. I discuss this question because I wish to avoid having my version of the benefits received argument as the basis for political obligation confused with an argument for political obligation based upon gratitude. Indeed, in my view, it is perfectly acceptable to contend that *ingratitude* is a justified citizen orientation to even good authority, or authority to which a citizen should have a strong obligation. I will explain this view in the pages that follow.

A. D. M. Walker avoids predicating political obligation as an obligation of gratitude upon an analogy between political and familial relationships. Where familial relationships are the guide for political obligation one should respect the state for the same reasons and in the same way one respects one's father. But since these relationships are quite different, making the familial relationship the model for the political is seen by Walker, and I think rightly so, as an error. As he says, the "appeal to the relationship between parents and children does nothing to show that among any obligations of gratitude a citizen may have to the state, there will be, specifically, an obligation to obey the law."[26] Instead, a political obligation by citizens to the state should be based upon a "general principle of gratitude."[27] Here the notion of gratitude presumes a principle of reciprocation between the citizen and the state as the basis for establishing political obligations.

This principle is built from certain attitudes held by citizens; namely, that people who receive benefits "*appreciate* the benefit and have *goodwill* and *respect* for the benefactor."[28] Thus, a show of gratitude displays a desire to communicate to the benefactor that one is grateful for what the benefactor provides, but also a show of gratitude demonstrates a desire to help the benefactor if and when the benefactor falls on hard times.[29] The principle of reciprocation in this case is located within an attitude of respect and goodwill for benefactors and an appreciation for the benefits one receives from benefactors.[30] Consequently, even though Walker does not make the ordinary familial relationship the basis for understanding political obligation based on gratitude, he seems to make another kind of ordinary relationship the basis for political obligation, the relationship of friends or strangers who provide important help to others.

Walker takes the view that knowledge of what the notion of gratitude means in ordinary settings of this sort can act as the basis for developing an account of political obligation based on gratitude. Here, the state is like a friend or a stranger offering assistance to a person in need. And if we think it right on principle to show the friend or the stranger respect and goodwill, then how can we act consistently if we do not show the same respect and goodwill to the state? All that remains to make the argument complete, then, is to demonstrate what it means to say we show respect and goodwill to the state. For Walker we should use the same guidelines we would use in showing goodwill to any benefactor. We are to show goodwill, to paraphrase Walker, by helping benefactors if they are in need or distress (so long as we can do so at no great cost to ourselves), by complying with reasonable requests, and by not acting against a benefactor's interests or rights.[31] To violate these principles, says Walker, is to act with ingratitude.[32]

These principles of conduct are used by Walker in devising a political obligation of gratitude. For Walker, then, a show of gratitude ordinarily means that a person "who benefits from X has an obligation of gratitude not to act contrary to X's interests." By extension to political authority, because "every citizen has received benefits from the state," every citizen "has an obligation of gratitude not to act in ways that are contrary to the state's interests." Indeed, "non-compliance with the law is contrary to the state's interests." This means that "every citizen has an obligation of gratitude to comply with the law," or else citizens would threaten the state's interests.[33] In this view no citizen is ever justified in violating particular laws if the citizen receives benefits from the state, for in violating the law the citizen shows ingratitude to the state by harming its interests.

But basing political obligation upon an obligation of gratitude leaves the major problem of political obligation unresolved. The reason for this contention is that the notion of gratitude in normal use does not suggest how to resolve the matter of conflicting loyalties. Walker's approach seems to indicate that when one makes gratitude the basis for respecting the state's authority, then it is the case that any time one benefits from the state one must respect its authority. But this imperative overlooks the fact that citizens may benefit from nonstate associations too. The view of gratitude Walker provides does not suggest that one should avoid accepting the authority of nonstate associations if one benefits from them. The problem here is what should a citizen do when the demands of the state conflict with the demands of a nonstate association and citizens cannot show gratitude to one without being ingracious to the other? This is the real domain as well as dilemma of political obligation.

The benefits received view developed in this chapter is designed to demonstrate the basis for citizens having the ability to resolve this dilemma. Moreover, on the view of obligation found in the benefits received view, it is important that the state provide essential benefits in order for citizens to have a strong obligation to authority. But given this position, then, it is clear to citizens that ingratitude may be a justifiable position for liberal citizens to hold. Let me explain.

To manifest ingratitude is for a citizen to say when confronted with a state-nonstate conflict that despite the state's provision of benefits, a citizen still does not have to respect the state's rights and abide by all of its laws. Is this action acceptable? Walker would suggest that it is not. He supports this contention in part by arguing against those who say that violations of particular laws may be so "trivial" that they do not "qualify as [causing] damage to the state's interests."[34] He claims that it is necessary to look at individual acts of violation not in isolation, but collectively. A single act of lawbreaking when placed in a setting with many other possible acts could when added up lead to seriously damaging consequences for the state. "There is no denying that collectively the activities of lawbreakers inflict severe damage on the vital interests of the state."[35]

But as I have already intimated (and will more fully argue in chapters 2, 4, and 5), the liberal state maintains itself as a liberal state, in part, when it is able to tolerate disobedience carried out as part of a form of civil protest to particular state policies. Certainly noncivil forms of protest may be viewed as causing serious harm to the state, leading the state to believe itself justified in protecting itself against noncivil acts even if it must itself act in a manner that is illiberal. In this case the liberal state might threaten its own liberal character to protect its ability to govern. Neither liberal citizens nor officials in a liberal state are presumed to want this outcome. So it is in the interest of both to maintain a basis for a strong obligation. In this setting, when citizens protest state policies, even those of a state that provides basic rights and liberties, they may decide to violate particular laws. Of course, the state's interest is harmed by this action too, for violating the law may cause the state to divert resources from other vital areas to resolve the problems the lawbreaking creates for it. Still, in this case the harm done to the liberal state is but a slight insult, and ingratitude here is not the basis for considering that the citizen intends to nor in fact seriously does harm the state. Public officials in this setting must develop the maturity and self-discipline to tolerate slights of this sort if they are to maintain the liberal state.

On the argument presented in this chapter, then, there are two occasions in which ingratitude can be justifiably manifested by citizens toward the state. In the first, ingratitude carries a potential for extreme harm that the state resists, and in the second the harm is minor and must be tolerated. In either case, ingratitude is seen as potentially justifiable. Thus, regarding the first instance, it is understood that the state provides many benefits that help to sustain the life of its citizens. There are normal benefits that states are expected to provide, benefits like security, defense from external enemies, provision of a food and water supply, the rule of law, and so on. But then there are other benefits which I have called major or essential. These benefits are special because they help to maintain society as a cooperative setting among diverse elements. In particular, the essential benefit of a liberal society is the provision of liberties in a way that secures both elements of its culture, individualist and communalist, in a manner beneficial to each. This benefit is provided when the state is organized to make possible an enlarged citizen–state culture, as explained in the next several chapters. In this setting the state creates the basis for expecting from citizens a strong obligation, and if a state provides ordinary benefits but fails to provide the essential ones too, then citizens are justified in manifesting their sense of political obligation in a manner that shows ingratitude to the state. Here, citizens may say that despite the fact that the state provides an opportunity to have good food, water, and the rule of law, it does not provide rights and liberties in a way that makes possible an enlarged culture and thus it cannot protect both the individualist and communalist tendencies of the society. (A more detailed discussion of this point is provided in my discussion of William Galston's liberalism at the conclusion of chapter 3.) Citizens may then be justified in protesting state policies (and manifesting ingratitude) by resorting to tactics that threaten the state's authority. And in showing ingratitude through manifestations of noncivil conduct, citizens realize that they will be perceived as causing severe harm to the state which provides ordinary benefits they do make use of. But they believe themselves justified because they want to make sure that in the future the ordinary benefits are arranged to provide rights and liberties in a way that secures an enlarged culture.

The second way a citizen is justified in manifesting ingratitude arises, as just developed, when the citizen concludes that because the state does provide essential benefits, citizens owe it a strong obligation. But because a citizen disagrees with a particular law, he decides to protest that law by disobeying it. In Walker's view of gratitude a citizen who receives benefits should show gratitude by respecting the laws of the state. Still, citizens with a strong obligation may violate laws so long as they use tactics that do not threaten its authority, and thus they must choose civil forms of protest. If this form of ingratitude were met with state oppression of those manifesting it, the right of citizens to challenge authority to justify its policies would be threatened. As a result, a central feature of liberal regimes, the nurturing of the critically reflective citizen, would be denied as well. But, in a liberal state, one worthy of a strong obligation, actions of individuals in protesting particular laws and in promoting the critically reflective qualities of citizens are not a danger to the state. Indeed, if the liberal state felt seriously threatened by this activity and acted to suppress it, the state would be unable to provide a basis for an enlarged culture and the critically reflective citizen who thrives in this culture. Then citizens would be justified in holding a weak obligation to authority, using noncivil forms of protest to display their ingratitude.

Finally, Walker says that "gratitude is not a species of fairness."[36] This means that "appeals to gratitude . . . are not appeals to fairness."[37] A state can provide certain benefits without at the same time providing those benefits that signify conformity to a practice of reciprocity "in which both beneficiary and benefactor are participants."[38] But obligations made in Walker's fashion make gratitude an untenable basis for political obligations. As argued here, reciprocity and fairness are a pivotal basis for obligation. This means that if the state provides essential benefits, it must presume citizen allegiance, or otherwise citizens would be acting in a way to undermine a structure of central importance to their own interests. And this would violate common sense. Similarly, if the state asked citizens to accept without question a scheme that did not provide essential benefits, then once again citizens would be asked to give uncritical support to the state, and in this case, they would forfeit their right to be critically reflective citizens. The only citizens who could maintain relationships of this sort would be ones who accepted an "iron fist" approach to governance, and this kind of society would have little concern to provide rights and liberties for the development of persons. In this case, to maintain a sense of obligation from gratitude would require liberal citizens to abandon the idea of the liberal state protecting a society suitable for critically reflective citizens with respect for diversity.

In conclusion, the benefits received argument, which embodies the principle of fairness as the basis for a strong obligation, does not make a sense of gratitude the basis for obligation. To do so is to base political obligation on a ground that violates the liberal character of the liberal state. Liberal citizens who are critically reflective persons would not be prone to take this course.

V. CHAPTER SUMMARIES

The problem remains then: What is the basis for saying that one is justifiably obligated to the state in a strong sense, especially in the face of nonstate obligations which one also feels? As just indicated, I argue that a state is owed a strong obligation when its commitment to rights and liberties works to secure an enlarged culture. The justification for the central importance of an enlarged culture rests upon an accommodationist argument which has two parts. In the first part (chapter 2, the general philosophical justification for enlarged thought), I argue against a perfectionist view of political argument found in Plato and Kant. This view presumes that there exist key notions of right that are the foundation of all political arguments. For perfectionists, all concepts which are used in political arguments pertaining either to the basic structure of the society or to particular political issues can be logically related to each other and to the key ideas of right to form a coherent system of concepts. But in practice, perfectionist systems prove useless for making political judgments of actual issues, and thus the only basis for making political judgments is through a form of enlarged discourse, wherein citizens holding different views of how best to approach a question test their views against those they disagree with and work to accommodate their differences. Ironically, the basis for the concept of the enlarged culture can be found in Kant's *Third Critique*.

Further support for this general philosophical argument is provided in chapter 2 by reference to the writings of Adam Smith. Kant's view of enlarged thought stipulates the rules people must follow to think in enlarged terms. But in politics, people often are motivated by passions of the most intense sort. And to think in enlarged terms, these passions must be diminished in intensity. But will people find enlarged thinking natural, if they must deny the intensity of their passions? Smith demonstrates that the impartial spectator, who would follow Kant's rules, is motivated by a major sentiment, the sentiment inherent in an enlarged culture, a sympathy for others. As a result of sympathy, people are enabled to see worth in others' views and to consider them carefully as they test their own views against others'. Sympathy as a major sentiment does not deny other passions, so much as it, as Smith says, "cools" other passions so that they do not hinder the ability to form views by comparing them to those held by others, ultimately with the hope of achieving a "balance" among the opposing views. Moreover, sympathy directs citizen concerns to what is the major standpoint embedded in an enlarged culture, a concern that the claims of those alleging that the society harms them are addressed and resolved. Kant demonstrates the intellectual structure of an enlarged culture, Smith demonstrates why such a culture would be emotionally satisfying, and later chapters build on both to demonstrate how an enlarged culture is the foundation for a discourse of fairness.

Finally, liberal society is predicated on the continued support by citizens of certain basic concepts like equality and liberty. In the absence of a perfectionist framework, these concepts might lose their significance, since, in this case, they would support a political system which often sustained contradictory moral positions. That is why, for instance, values like liberty and equality are often in conflict and that is why different interpretations of these values compete for public acceptance. Still, these ideals regain their significance in an enlarged culture. For in an enlarged culture, as citizens seek to find the best application of a basic concept in resolving a practical issue, citizens must carefully consider one another's views, and by doing so, the understanding develops that as diverse views pertaining to how to maintain a major ideal are considered, that ideal's significance is made more important to the culture, even if as a result of the enlarged discourse an integrated system of concepts does not emerge. This understanding helps to sustain support for those ideals that held to maintain the liberal society.

But the general philosophical argument for an enlarged culture does not explain the practical motivation people must have in order to have a desire to sustain this standard. Thus in the second part of the argument for the enlarged thought standard, developed in chapter 3, I hope to explain the practical motivation people would have for supporting an enlarged culture. It is necessary to discuss the hopes and conflicts in a liberal society faced by liberal citizens, and then show that given both the hopes and conflicts, citizens would make the enlarged culture standard a basis for a strong obligation. My approach to this objective is to demonstrate that for the ideal liberal citizen, who is also a critically reflective citizen, there is a need to find a way to accommodate both strains of the liberal schism discussed in the early part of this chapter, individualism and communalism. To this end, the critically reflective citizen knows that even if in his private life he is prone to promote one strain over the other, in his public conduct he must refuse to embark upon a course that would lead to the establishment of one strain in the extreme sense. He reasons that to do so would lead to both a denial of the significance of rights and liberties for the development of persons, and possibly a complete refusal to permit citizens to have these rights and liberties for any reason. Further, an extreme expression of a given strain would contradict the basic values and nature of that strain. Thus there is a need to avoid extremes, and the enlarged culture is embraced because it provides a way to do so. The argument of chapter 3 concludes by demonstrating why the enlarged culture standard is even more a basis for a practical motivation for a strong obligation than aspects typically used to justify political obligation such as the rule of law, social peace, freedom from want, and so forth.

In chapter 4 I move from a discussion of the problem of political obligation and the search for a standard to justify a strong sense of obligation to an effort to make applications of the enlarged culture standard to assess individual moral quandaries and the worth of political and social arrangements in a liberal regime. From chapter 4 to the end of the book, then, my interest is in demonstrating how this standard can be used to address satisfactorily real problems.

In chapter 4, I point out that liberal states both support the freedom of conscience and the need for citizens to act from conscience, but liberal states will at times penalize citizens for doing so. Is this not a contradiction that in fact should erode a strong obligation to the liberal state? I argue against this view, provided certain conditions are met. Citizens of conscience who see the state take positions contrary to their own view of right still must have a strong obligation to the state, and thus practice civil forms of protest to laws they object to, if the state on the whole maintains an enlarged culture. There are two reasons for this position. The first is that conscience, as a human activity, only survives in a cooperative society. In this setting, citizens sustain the practices necessary to maintain the life activities of those committed to live by their conscience. But a cooperative society is only possible where there is an enlarged culture. For in this culture, citizen experience teaches the importance of upholding the various responsibilities and burdens that are the basis for maintaining a cooperative society. This point is further developed in chapter 7 in the discussion of the social learning process that supports the discourse on fairness. Further, the authoritative base for conscience is the kind of discourse and thinking sustained by an enlarged culture. In a liberal society traditional sources of conscience like religion or natural law are supplemented with, and perhaps even supplanted by, an enlarged culture. Once again, if the state protects an enlarged culture, it protects the possibility and importance of freedom of conscience in a liberal society, even if at times it must act to deny particular positions held by persons of conscience.

In chapter 5, my intent is to demonstrate those characteristics which liberal states must have in order for citizens to say that the state nurtures an enlarged culture between itself and its citizens. In addressing this question I assume that citizens will not have direct access to the policy-making process, and thus to a large extent they will be ruled without having a chance to rule in turn. How is a state to manifest an enlarged culture in this context? I discuss various possibilities, including a form of representative politics that is suitable to establishing an enlarged culture. My point is that in a state which does not permit direct citizen involvement in making laws, there must be a strong challenge tradition. This tradition allows citizens to create an enlarged relationship between themselves and those who make and implement policies. Moreover, I emphasize the central importance of public reason, which is a political form of enlarged thinking that state officials must use in order to provide an atmosphere conducive to the development of critically reflective citizens.

In chapter 6, I distinguish my view of an enlarged culture from those found in Carole Pateman and Benjamin Barber. These writers make participatory democracy the basis for an enlarged citizen-state culture, but I contend that this relationship can be obtained within the legitimate, liberal state which does not have the participatory setting these writers desire. This outcome is possible as long as there is a tradition of public officials acting to resist the power of important political groups so that the concerns of all the citizens can be properly considered and the solutions to these concerns implemented. What secures this possibility is the challenge tradition and public officials who are committed to maintaining constitutional balance among the executive, legislative, and judicial branches of government.

In chapter 7, I discuss the nature of the social learning process that a liberal state must have. Without a social learning process, citizens might not consider the state's liberal qualities at all important, and then the liberal state might be transformed in a way that threatened its best, liberal characteristics. In this case, the issue of political obligation would become moot. The question, then, concerns the nature of the social learning process that teaches the importance of basic rights and liberties. Here I discuss aspects of Rawls's theory of moral development in *A Theory of Justice* in developing the basic parameters for the useful liberal social learning process. I elicit from this theory two key points, which I think must be established in order to make Rawls's theory of moral development work. First, I claim that people learn to respect rights and liberties only when the latter are used to achieve a cooperative setting in society that secures self-respect for the citizens. Second, people understand society in these terms only if the society is able, in its institutions, to teach people to think about society in enlarged terms, a point of view which makes fairness a critical objective. In this view, the central standpoint of the liberal citizen is made clear: He or she must listen to and address the claims of those who argue that they have been harmed by the cooperative arrangements. Moreover, public officials understand that citizens expect that they conduct the business of the discourse on fairness, too.

The consequence of a citizen-state relationship grounded in the discourse of fairness is a society where citizens are influenced by the discourse of fairness to appreciate the various contributions others must make to maintain society as a cooperative setting. But just as important, citizens understand that the social arrangement must be modified at times to include within the orbit of the cooperative setting those not presently covered by it. An enlarged understanding is shown to be critical at both the political and social levels to protect the cooperative ethos of society.

In chapter 8, I maintain that an enlarged culture, so essential to protecting the cooperative arrangement of society, cannot be sustained if there are serious social antagonisms caused by an absence of a commitment to provide the elements of essential material decency to all citizens. But if the enlarged culture is protected, then citizens have a basis for resolving conflicts that arise over the "better" or "best" cooperative social form. Further, an enlarged culture resists historical tendencies to reinstitute various forms of bigotry that threaten respect for diversity and undermine the search for a "better" or "best" way to maintain and protect it. Thus, for the sake of an enlarged culture, I argue for a political agenda that makes as a central priority the provision of basic material goods in a way that secures a decent life for all citizens. To make this argument, I refer to Michael Walzer's *Spheres of Justice*.

The final chapter makes the point that an enlarged culture is neither so thin that it becomes the basis for value relativism nor so thick that it mandates notions of the good that all citizens must learn to accommodate to. In its essence, this public culture seeks to secure the basis for the life of the critically reflective citizen who makes as the basis of obligation a state that secures rights and liberties for all in a setting that allows for the development and respect of all persons.

2

The Enlarged Culture
and Obligation:
The General Argument

I. LEGITIMACY AND OBLIGATION

In the last chapter, I suggested that a state that is legitimate by virtue of providing basic rights and liberties may only sustain a weak obligation, and thus additional justifications are necessary for a legitimate, liberal state to justify a strong obligation from citizens. To clarify the grounds for a strong obligation, I first describe, in this section, the nature of the legitimate, liberal state and demonstrate how this form of government, with its support for basic rights and liberties, highlights the importance to liberal societies of a critically reflective citizen body. To maintain this kind of citizenship, an enlarged culture becomes a necessary addition to the state's commitment to provide rights and liberties. My argument for this position is framed within a discussion of Kant, which follows this section. This discussion of Kant is designed to demonstrate that liberal citizens need an enlarged culture if they are to make critically reflective political judgments that embody another major idea of liberal regimes, the idea of respect for persons.

Liberal legitimacy is predicated on a concept of the moral and political principles of a given culture that both citizens and state officials mutually accept.[1] For instance, and here I stress what seem to be accepted canons of the contemporary liberal regime, there is a concern for making possible the development and sense of self-worth of persons by securing fundamental public rights and liberties for all citizens. Provision of basic rights and liberties is a standard tenet of liberal regimes, and writers like John Rawls, Richard Flathman,

Ronald Dworkin, Alan Gewirth, and others reflect in their thought this basic cultural agreement as to the nature of liberal regimes.[2] The basic rights and liberties include, for instance, freedom of speech, conscience, association, press, religion, privacy, and thought. In addition, citizens are to have equal opportunity to influence the policy-making process (the liberty of political participation), due process of law, protection of the right of private property, and the right to challenge authority to justify its decisions.

Citizens understand that public officials who make policy decisions are often faced with great difficulties as they seek to make policies that at the same time protect basic rights and liberties. These difficulties arise from the fact that the rights and liberties themselves may have to be ordered or ranked in importance, with some liberties and rights being defined on some occasions as more important than others. The scheme that orders rights and liberties reflects certain societal approaches to the way different issues should be addressed. This means that on some occasions where two liberties are in conflict, say speech and private property, the former will have priority, and on other occasions the latter will have priority. For instance, the right of private property has priority in situations where one claims the right of free speech entitles one to destroy another's property in order to bring to the attention of the public "supposed crimes" that the holders of the property in question are alleged to have committed. On other occasions the right of speech supersedes in importance the right of private property. For instance, it would not be acceptable to claim that owing to a person's ownership of property one's views should be permitted expression whereas a person without wealth must not be accorded the same privilege. A citizen should have the full right of speech just by virtue of being a citizen.

As another example, at times the freedom of association and speech may have to be given a lower priority than the freedom of thought, as is the case when mob rule would threaten the right of persons to investigate ideas without interference. Here freedom of thought, which includes the right of others to hear, must be given priority over the freedom of speech demanded by those who seek to use their voices to shout down the speakers at a meeting where ideas are being investigated.

Further, political decisions which arrange these liberties and rights are controversial, and it is likely that disagreements will emerge on how best to proceed. To avoid creating a situation in which citizens think there is no prospect for revising these decisions, liberal societies hope to provide leeway for citizen "corrections" of government policy by ensuring that political power is distributed across the main institutions of government and not concentrated in a single governing body or in the hands of a ruling group. For it is presumed that where power is not shared among governing bodies like the executive, legislative, and judicial branches, the state's authority would be used to undermine an atmosphere in which citizen challenges can take place and can actually result in the revision of state decisions. If there is a bias toward making one set of rights of higher importance, the bias is to make the rights associated with the right to challenge primary. Otherwise, the political system becomes unable to create an environment in which citizens have what Flathman refers to as autonomy and the latter in part consists in persons making "critical assessments of the norms and rules of her society." Flathman, following James Fishkin, speaks of a need in a liberal society for a "self-justifying society; a society in which the citizenry is steadily concerned to justify to itself what it collectively and collectedly does."[3]

To maintain the possibility of a self-justificatory society, there must be an agreement concerning the minimum standards for the distribution of basic goods like education, health care, economic opportunities, and so forth. Where these goods are not distributed fairly citizens will not trust the basic liberties (or government officials who uphold them) to work in ways to avoid dangerous concentrations of power. At the same time, an agreement on minimums does not remove the sources of major disagreements over policy. For even where it is clear that necessary goods are supplied to citizens on a basis that provides opportunities for a decent life, citizens may nonetheless have wide differences of opinion as to the "better" or "best" distribution of essential goods. (I will discuss and develop this point further in chapter 8.)

The point to emphasize, then, is that even though the basic rights and liberties, as Rawls claims, are permanent and unqualified goods,[4] the quest to realize these freedoms is always located within controversies that pertain to the "better" or "best" distribution of basic goods. In general, the question of "better" or "best" presumes that whereas citizens can agree on the nature of what constitutes a decent form of life, still, they are constantly discussing what the "better" or "best" form should be. Thus even if we can agree that society's resources should be distributed to make possible certain levels of education, medical care, welfare, and security, there are still likely to be major differences of opinion concerning the "better" or "best" distribution of these goods. At issue are matters that pertain to how best to organize society so that it makes possible the development of self-worth of persons.

This concern always reaffirms the central importance in a liberal society of those liberties that permit citizens to be critically reflective of their society's efforts in providing the basis for citizen self-worth. This means as well that citizens must retain an ability to make reforms in a direction that mirrors their critical reflections. Moreover, as a consequence of these reflections, citizens may conclude that a state that acts legitimately (by securing basic rights and liberties for all persons) may not form policies that symbolize a basis for citizens justifying a strong obligation to liberal authority. Indeed, citizens may use their critically reflective capacities that the rights and liberties protect and adjudge the existing system of rights and liberties as lacking in moral worth. In this case other obligations emanating not from the state, but from nonstate domains may emerge as stronger than those associated with the state. This situation may be the occasion for citizens having a weak obligation to the state.

II. KANT AND THE ENLARGED CULTURE

So what must liberal states do to earn citizen respect and thus secure a strong sense of citizen obligation to its laws and to its authority? The argument made throughout the book is that a strong sense of obligation is justified where a legitimate, liberal state maintains an enlarged relationship between itself and its citizens. The first stage of the argument takes place in this chapter, and the second part, the search for a practical motivation to support an enlarged culture, takes place in the next chapter.

In the first stage, the general philosophical justification developed in this chapter, I contend that the reason enlarged thinking is so vital is that critical assessments of society cannot be base solely on a form of reasoning which presumes that political life can be governed by a set of shared principles integrated into a kind of Platonic system that becomes the basis for making political judgments about important matters affecting public life. In a Platonic system there is a definitive principle of right, in the case of *The Republic*, the ideal of justice, and all judgments pertaining to education, law, or even the nature of what we consider private matters like marriage, religion, and parent-child interactions should be made in such a way as to embody this principle. Ultimately what should emerge is a system of integrated concepts all connected to each other in a complementary fashion, and all connected back to the supreme governing principle, the ideal of justice.[5] The ultimate authority for this system is not simply its integrated quality, but it is what makes this integrated quality possible: a form of pure reason which can discover objective and universally valid principles of truth. Pure reason is able to determine objective principles for judgment because it is not distorted by experience or emotion, factors which cloud understanding and prevent reason from determining objective principles that can be the foundation of an integrated system of concepts.

Kant, in the The Critique of Pure Reason, understood his effort to be in part a search for the first principles which help persons to comprehend the workings of nature. Kant associates himself with Plato in this regard, and he says, "what to us is an ideal, was to Plato's language an *Idea of a divine mind*, an individual object present to its pure intuition, the most perfect of every kind of possible beings, and the archetype of all phenomenal copies."[6] Kant in the same section indicates that he too expects to use this approach in studying ethics. "Moral concepts are not entirely pure concepts of reason, because they rest on something empirical, pleasure or pain. Nevertheless, with regard to the principle by which reason imposes limits on freedom which in itself is without laws, these moral concepts . . . may well serve as examples of pure concepts of reason."[7] Rational persons can use practical reason to discern ethical and political concepts or maxims that have universal form. These maxims have a similar character in that they contain as the central concern the objective idea of respect for persons. Taken together, the maxims of ethics and politics can be joined into a system of concepts all systematically connected to the key principle of practical reason, respect for persons.

Had Kant been successful in pursuing this course, then he would have shown how his main moral principle, respect for persons, could be made the centerpiece of his ethics and politics. Indeed, as I demonstrate in the next several sections, Kant hoped to show that the various institutions, sectors, and laws of the society should be formed in order to maintain consistency with this main principle. success would not only demonstrate conceptual consistency and the role of practical reason in obtaining it, but it would show the significance and importance of the leading idea of his thought, respect for persons, to politics and ethics.

But the reality of modern politics, as I argue in the next several sections, is that a thought system of this sort symbolizes a vision of a perfect intellectual order that fails to provide a practical basis for making political judgments. In place of a perfectionist framework, citizens predicate judgments upon a process of enlarged thinking.

Here citizens follow certain rules for public discourse that help people to formulate their opinions by carefully considering and testing their views against the wide diversity of views that exist. Citizens have confidence in opinions formed in accordance with the rules for enlarged thinking because the distorting elements to clear thought, like bias, prejudice, and emotion, are greatly reduced. These distorting aspects make it difficult to derive judgments based upon the best possible understanding that people can have of situations. And when distortions are reduced, as is the case when people follow the rules of enlarged thought, citizens can have confidence in their judgments, even if they do not lead to or result from an integrated, Platonic system of concepts.

Further, to make enlarged thinking the basis of political judgment helps to demonstrate the significance of the notion of respect for persons to politics. The justification for this crucial idea in liberal thought does not depend upon success of a form of reasoning which uses this idea to achieve conceptual consistency across the domains of ethics and politics. Rather, where enlarged thinking is seen as a necessary basis for political judgment, then to actually engage in it, respect for persons must be maintained in the guise of citizens' willingness to form opinions by testing their own views against the views of others. As further argued, this enterprise requires that citizens sustain a sympathetic attitude toward each other, an emotional dimension of an enlarged discourse discussed not by Kant but by Adam Smith. In any event, the value of respect for persons retains its significance in a liberal culture precisely because enlarged thinking is seen as so critical a dimension of this culture.[8]

III. KANT'S EFFORTS TO TIE ETHICS TO POLITICS

Kant's main ethical principle is the categorical imperative, which says that people should "act only on a maxim by which you can will that it, at the same time, should become a general law."[9] As a consequence, Kant hoped to build a system of concepts of right by making all maxims for conduct be part of a larger system of maxims, each of which could be said to possess categorical form.

Further, forming maxims for how to guide personal conduct is a function of a person's ability to use one's rational faculties to test the worth of a proposed maxim by determining if the maxim has the form of a universal law of nature and thus could be willed by all rational persons. If the maxim has universal form, then it is a duty that must be obeyed. Maxims are "givens" of practical reason. Ethical truth does not derive from a conversation or agreement among persons discussing the question of how best to act. Rather these truths are already at hand, and they must be discovered by a process of practical reasoning. Ethical truth emerges from the self-reflection of rational persons, who ask if a proposed maxim is one which all rational persons would subscribe to because each would see that it has the status of a law of nature. Thus, in formulating a maxim, Kant asks us to determine if,

> the action which you propose should take place by a law of nature of which you yourself were a part, you could regard it as possible through your will. Everyone does, in fact, decide by this rule whether actions are morally good or bad. Thus people ask: if one belonged to such an order of things that anyone would allow himself to deceive when he thought it to his advantage, or felt justified in shortening his life as soon as he were thoroughly weary of it, or looked with complete indifference on the needs of others, would he assent of his own will to being a member of such an order of things?[10]

In approaching ethical questions in this way, one finds that conduct should be oriented toward the core principle of treating all persons, including oneself, as an end and not solely as a means.[11] Because this principle has universal form, it is a categorical command or duty that suggests the need to be committed to a variety of ethical imperatives or maxims which embody the core principle, including the duty not to lie, the duty against avarice, the duty to "cultivate one's natural powers," and the duty of beneficence or the "maxim to make the happiness of others an end for oneself."[12] These duties, like the others which Kant discusses in "The Metaphysical Principles of Virtue" are part of a system of maxims which are unified by virtue of the fact that they all embody the categorical principle to treat others as ends.

Kant also hopes to rest his politics on the categorical principle to treat others as ends. Politics can "pay homage to morality" in part through juridical maxims which are viewed as embodying Kant's great categorical principle.[13] The only difference between ethical and juridical maxims (which Kant also refers to as ethical and juridical laws) is that ethical maxims are held by persons through an internally willed commitment while juridical maxims may have to be imposed externally by the force of state law and authority. Kant says in discussing maxims of conduct that "insofar as they are directed to mere external actions and their legality, they are called *juridical*; but when, in addition, they demand that these laws themselves be the determining grounds of actions, then they are *ethical*. Accordingly we say: agreement with juridical laws constitutes the *legality* of action, whereas agreement with ethical ones constitute its *morality*."[14]

Lurking behind the distinction between the juridical and the ethical is acceptance of the fact that even if people have the capacity for moral knowledge, they still often act from motives of self-interest. Kant says that "from such crooked wood as man is made of, nothing perfectly straight can be built."[15] For this reason, then, the law which embodies moral objectives will require a state which can impose them coercively. Patrick Riley is right to argue that for Kant, citizens in acting as the legal system requires act morally but from nonmoral motives. Riley says, "The *Critique of Judgment*—the final *Critique*—reveals public legal justice as the single most important strand of a culture that also embraces art. science and the development of skill. Culture and particularly politics . . . is '*for*' the legal realization of some moral ends (such as peace) which good will would attain were it not for a pathological weakness of the flesh."[16]

The main principle of Kant's legal system, and also of his ethics, that people are to be treated as ends, is rendered for politics as the requirement to promote equal freedom. The freedom principle says that "every action is just [right] that in itself or in its maxims is such that the freedom of will of each can coexist together with the freedom of everyone in accordance with universal law."[17] Coercion is seen as removing the "hindrances" to freedom by ensuring that people act in ways toward others that are respectful of their freedom, and in doing so people would act as required by the principle to treat others as ends.[18] Thus the legal system requires citizens not to kill, steal, and so forth, and in not doing these things, citizens act morally even if from nonmoral reasons.

Politics, then, is "instrumental," as Riley says, to morality.[19] But if this is the case, then Kant must be seen as taking a step which potentially threatens his effort to build a perfectionist system. This contention can best be made in discussing Kant's framework for constitutional government.[20] His view requires three branches, each with their separate functions. The executive makes commands which "are not laws, but ordinances and decrees, because they involve decisions about particular cases." The legislature "cannot at the same time be the ruler [the executive] for the ruler himself is subject to the law and through it is obligated to another, the sovereign [the legislature]."[21] The executive carries out and therefore always must act within the law established by the legislature. Finally, the judicial system, in addition to hearing criminal cases, must resolve controversies involving the application of the law with respect to disagreements over property.

Since people alleging that a harm has been committed against them make their claims against either the executive that applies the law or the legislature that makes it, neither branch should be allowed to resolve these controversies, because they are interested parties, and they might judge unfairly (or as Kant says they would do an "injustice" to) the persons alleging that the actions of the government harm them.

Seen as a whole, the constitution establishes a system in which there are separate centers of authority. Because public officials, like any other citizens, may become corrupted to the point where they would use their position to promote only their own interests, it is necessary to place limits on their authority. People may have a capacity to know the nature of right, but for the most part, in their actions, they may be guided solely by self-interest concerns anyway. Given this fact, political activity in this setting inevitably comes to reflect a Madisonian balance of power system, in which, owing to the fact that each separate part can veto the actions of the whole, it becomes necessary for each of the parts to strive for agreement if any government action is to be possible at all. Ironically, then, a government system designed to prevent the pursuit of unlimited power by a few requires public officials to respect different interests and work to find a common basis for action among them.

This would mean, in practical terms, that the separate branches and the different interests represented therein must make an effort to accommodate one anothers' objectives through a process of bargaining and compromise. It is clear that Kant had no intention of developing his politics in these terms. Riley's analysis rightly leads to the conclusion that the basis for action in Kant should be a principle of moral right possessing universal validity, which all rational people support, and it is this principle, and not the result of a discourse seeking a compromise among diverse interests, that should be the cornerstone of all action. Riley summarizes admirably Kant's teleology as a "single realm in which politics, law, and eternal peace, as facets of a culture that also embraces art and science, fit in a remarkably comprehensive scheme based on a 'purposive unity' as the 'highest' unity."[22]

But if the discourse of politics were to become accommodationist, then instead of conceptual consistency existing at the base of his politics, a consistency in which the law always was fashioned to reflect a coherent ethical system, the law might have to embrace many contradictory moral purposes that people would have to learn to accept in order to maintain the possibility of a decision process based on bargaining and honest compromise. To accept this reality, a reality which is implied by the concessions to the real nature of human beings found in Kant's view of constitutional government, Kant's politics would have to be rewritten to make room for what today is a modern fact of life; namely, that modern politics is based on a concern to constantly attempt to accommodate the intentions of people who have contradictory understandings about the best way to approach a common issue. The grounds for holding different opinions might be attributed to many things, like one's place in society or government, or simply one's sentiments. Nonetheless, the fact that people hold different views on matters of importance makes it difficult to expect a unified moral system to emerge. In consequence, the legal system would have to manifest the need to tolerate diverse approaches to common issues and to find some way to resolve them. Thus, people would search for a way to reconcile their differences, but the result of the search might be a legal system which sustains opposing moral views on many issues.

Kant's freedom principle can be understood, at first glance, as demonstrating tolerance for this possibility. If people are to be equally free, then they must not be interfered with during the course of pursuing their life plans, and thus the common laws against theft, murder, and so forth help to secure this possibility. Yet, the freedom to act for one's life plans presumes the possibility of there being some agreement on what constitutes reasonable manifestations of what it means to treat others as ends. But where there exist different conceptions as to what constitutes treatment of people as ends, the prospect of an integrated moral system that embodies the principle of respect for persons is threatened. For example, people who want abortion have one conception of what it means to treat people as ends, and those opposing abortion have another; those wanting more social welfare have a conception of treating people as ends that those wanting less social welfare do not share, and so on. How are issues of this type to be resolved?

Riley does not ask, as I wish to do, how Kant's political philosophy could be reconstructed to take into account this dimension of his politics without at the same time sacrificing the commitment to treat people as ends in themselves. In other terms, can there be an accommodationist discourse, which while not achieving the conceptual consistency Kant hopes for, still moves society in the direction of Kant's great moral principle to treat people as ends? Furthermore, why not reconstruct Kant's politics along these lines, especially when elements exist in his political philosophy to help accomplish this end? To move in this direction would demonstrate how the commitment to treat persons as ends could be achieved inside an accommodationist discourse, within both the basic political institutions of a liberal regime and an enlarged culture.

That scholars have recognized that Kant's thought does indeed contain the elements for a reconstruction along these lines is reflected in Ronald Beiner's work. He says that "Kant *might* have attempted to develop for politics a model of rational persuasion and judgment on his analysis of aesthetic judgment,"[23] but instead, he failed to do so. Of course, in defense of Beiner, there is no doubt that Kant would prefer conceptual consistency for grounding political judgments. This fact is seen in his discussion of the basic issues like private property, public welfare, punishment, the state's right to send citizens to war, and the rights of states during war. In each case, he posits what he understands to be universally valid maxims of right, which taken together work to maintain a state that can secure the freedom principle and its commitment to treating persons as ends.[24]

But again, the problem of sustaining this enterprise emerges for those issues where great controversy rages. Are there objective principles with universal validity at hand to resolve these issues? Kant hopes to find them and for deciding these matters Kant, as John Laursen points out, follows "the pattern of his works on morality" by providing a principle of transcendental right, which is "valid without demonstration," and this is the principle that "all actions relating to the rights of other men are unjust if their maxim is not compatible with publicity."[25] The principle of publicity says according to Kant that "if I cannot publicly avow it [a maxim] without inevitably exciting universal opposition to my project, the necessary and universal opposition which can be foreseen a priori is due only to the injustice with which the maxim threatens everyone."[26] Here Kant is saying that, as Laursen says, "virtually by definition any purposes or actions which can be carried out only with full public disclosure and public support are going to be legitimate."[27] The principle of publicity is then used to decide as Laursen says "contested issues like the right of rebellion, the binding effect of treaties, the justification of preemptive strikes, and the rights of strong countries."[28] Supposedly, then, in most public policy questions we do have a choice to make between competing maxims, and in choosing the maxim because it could be revealed without incurring public opposition, we have a definitive basis for conduct, a basis just as authoritative as practical reason supplies.

The principle of publicity presumes what practical reason holds; namely, that citizens should search for an objective concept that can be made the basis for making judgments about contested issues. The major problem with this approach is that in enunciating public maxims for particular issues, it is possible not to incur universal opposition, but still to incur enough opposition so as to make acceptance of a single maxim for judging an issue difficult to attain. What is clear in the real political world is that when one presents a particular concept as the basis for resolving an issue, one finds that some people agree, some disagree, and some have opinions that contain elements of agreement and disagreement.

Still, it is the case quite often that political judgments are based on maxims that the members of the society could and do support, much as Kant suggests with his notion of publicity. But in this case another problem may arise. The maxim chosen by the state to resolve a particular public policy question may be one which, while generally supported by the citizens, in a particular case conflicts with other maxims which some citizens would prefer to use. For instance, assume that in dealing with the question of how best to ensure blacks membership in a certain job category where they have previously been denied access, there is a general agreement to support the equal opportunity maxim. The government following this maxim then adopts a policy to implement an affirmative action program wherein jobs are set aside for blacks only. Other citizens may object on one of two grounds. These citizens may charge that this approach threatens individual freedom by denying people a chance to apply for the position if the only positions left open are those set aside for blacks. Further, it could be claimed by these people that when this freedom is interfered with, competition for hiring the best person does not exist, and this violates the idea that only the most competent people should get the job.

This conflict symbolizes the dilemma of political judgment in modern liberal states. A culture can be committed to all three maxims, but because it cannot agree on how to arrange their relationship, there is no integrated system of concepts, which demonstrates how all three are part of a harmonious system. Some might claim that in this case key maxims of a culture, like the three just elaborated, lose their significance, and as a consequence the culture loses its grounding. In the face of this problem, how can the significance of maxims like liberty, equality, and competence be preserved?

Kant's project can be viewed as concerned with this dilemma if we reinterpret the implications of his approach to politics. If, following Onora O'Neill,[29] Kant's politics is said to be predicated upon an enlarged discourse sustained by common principles, then in making political judgments citizens can still provide significance to the leading maxims of a liberal culture, even if it is the case that an integrated set of maxims, arrayed in Platonic fashion, appears to be impossible. An explanation of this approach to judgment is developed from Kant's *The Third Critique.*[30]

IV. KANT'S *THIRD CRITIQUE* AND POLITICAL
COMMUNICATION

The limitations of reason in making judgments just alluded to point to a disjunction between two types of judgments, determinative and reflective judgments. In determinative judgments, the setting of ethical judgments, practical reason supplies a principle, such as act beneficently to others or never lie, and this principle must be followed in determining what to do about a particular issue. Thus if I am faced with the prospect of telling the truth or lying to my draft board, I must tell the truth. If I am faced with the quandary of whether to visit a dear uncle who is near death or to see my favorite team play ball, the principle of beneficence should guide my actions.

In these cases there is an authoritative principle of practical reason which is determinative, and in determinative judgments "if the universal (the rule, the principle, the law) be given, the judgment which subsumes the particular under it . . . is determinant."[31] In contrast, reflective judgments deal with matters for which "the universal law has to be found."[32] Aesthetic judgments are one type of reflective judgment.[33] In aesthetic judgments a person says that something is beautiful and the basis for this judgment is the form of his own subjective perception of the particular event or object. There is no universal rule or concept, with the authority of reason, that can guide such judgments.

In matters pertaining to the beautiful, the concepts of practical reason are not relevant to providing a foundation for judgment. We do not say that it is always the case that what is ethically right is beautiful simply by virtue of the fact that something is ethically right. Instead, we say something is beautiful if it appears to be so to our subjective imagination. Moreover, because the beautiful depends on the subjective modes of perception of people, there are many different understandings and ideas of what is beautiful, and there is no single concept of the beautiful nor a science of aesthetics.

Despite the singularity of aesthetic judgments, these private judgments can be made public. People need to make their private judgments public in part because what gives pleasure to us (as aesthetic judgments do) is that we need to communicate our judgments to others. A person is inclined, says Kant, "to communicate his pleasure to others and . . . is not contented with an object if he cannot feel satisfaction in it in common with others." Indeed the need for communication is from an "original compact dictated by humanity itself."[34] Further, the process of communication presumes that it is natural for people to have contesting views, but as they share these views with each other, it is possible that they will reach agreements even in the absence of a determinant concept or system of concepts such as practical reason supplies.[35]

This communicative setting is constructed not from concepts (given by practical reason) which provide the basis for demonstrating how particulars should be judged, but by a capacity for (or faculty of) judgment or a "sensus communis" which, as the common possession of all, allows us to communicate our judgments by "comparing our judgments with the possible rather than the actual judgments of others."[36] By thinking in terms of the "possible" as opposed to the "actual," persons follow certain rules of understanding, rules that undergird the sensus communis.[37] The purpose in following these rules is to create a communicative setting that allows persons to learn from each others' views and to form their own judgments in a setting where this exchange is possible.

There are three essential maxims in Kant's rules for "common human understanding."[38] First, one should always "think for oneself." This is the maxim of "unprejudiced thought." To not think for oneself is to allow unexamined prejudice to dictate one's understandings, and it is to live by a maxim of "passive reason." Here one's thoughts are determined completely by others, and one manifests no critically evaluative posture of one's own.[39] According to the second rule of understanding, one must think in an "enlarged way."[40] In enlarged thinking, which I take to be the core dimension of the faculty of judgment, one searches for a standpoint that is beyond one's "subjective, private conditions of his own judgment" and moves toward a perspective built from an ability to place oneself "at the standpoint of others" so that one can form judgments by comparing and contrasting the views of others to one's own.[41] The final maxim is to "always think consistently."[42] One must think consistently or search for unity and coherence among viewpoints by constantly upholding in one's conduct the first two maxims. Once again, one is pushed by reason to find coherence in the world that one forms judgments of.

O'Neill says these rules of communication are acceptable because they "*could* be shared . . . by a plurality of at least partially free and rational beings."[43] In this sense, then, these rules are "morally required" maxims of communication.[44] O'Neill adds to the rules of the *sensus communis* others (which she correctly finds in Kant), such as an intention to avoid lying and a refusal to turn a discourse into a polemic where the only aim is victory in a debate.[45] Here, the communicative setting is predicated upon rules that all members accept as the basis for making and communicating judgments.

For my part, I call these rules the basis of an enlarged culture. To think in enlarged terms is to no longer allow passive forms of reason to dictate one's judgments. Enlarged thinking creates a point of view on problems which is more comprehensive than what one's own private understandings would permit, yet never so comprehensive as a pure form of reason, which seeks as the basis for judgment an integrated system of concepts based on a principle of truth. In ordinary debate about aesthetic matters, matters are not susceptible to being judged in terms of a system of integrated, objective principles, but these matters can be judged only through an enlarged understanding. Similarly, for political issues, citizens initiate the discussion from their own particular views of how best to proceed. If citizens were to remain mired in their own private understandings, they would not be able to test their views against those provided by others as the various parties work to find an agreement on how to approach an issue. O'Neill is correct to say in discussing enlarged thought that "there is no lofty position above the debate, as perhaps there might be if human reason had a transcendental source. There is only the position of one who strives to reach and understand the perspectives of others to communicate with rather than past them"[46]

Citizens in this setting form their judgments by comparing and contrasting their views to those held by others. In consequence, people are open to carefully consider the objections of others to their views, and from this activity it is possible for them to search for a consensus on the standards that should govern how particular instances should be judged. This is a "possible" as opposed to an "actual" form of judgment because it occurs in a world that is not completely enlightened, a world where enlarged thinking has yet to fully emerge and often people may resort to forms of thought which violate the Kantian rules of understanding. But that is not an inevitable outcome, and in an enlarged and enlightened culture citizens realize that to make judgments, which are necessary for their common survival, they must think in these "possible" terms.

The maxims of enlarged thinking are essential guides to conduct in this case not only because they appear to be rules which all "partially rational" persons would accept, but also because these rules enable citizens to share views and from this endeavor attempt to reach agreements on the standards that should be followed. Here the basis of the standards people accept is not practical reason itself, as in the case of ethical matters, where as a result of practical reason people are "given" the principles which have universal validity, but instead, the authority for the standards is a dialog that is guided by morally justified rules.

The practical implication for politics of this approach is important. For in a setting where people hold to certain general principles, like equality, liberty, rule of law, and so on, it is possible to ground these principles in an enlarged dialog and by doing so give these principles continued importance, even if it is the case that no integrated system of concepts emerges as a result of the judgments that are made as a result of an enlarged discourse.

To return to the example of equality of opportunity versus individual liberty, it is the case that both values are held simultaneously in our society, but as a result it is inevitable that one principle is seen as conflicting with the other, depending on how an individual defines his point of view. Thus as an enlarged dialog characterizes the search for how best to achieve equality, it is the case that people who favor the liberty dimension will find it difficult to fully support programs for equal opportunity that threaten their liberty. As a result of the policy process, not all the goals sought by those wanting full equality of opportunity can be met. Still, because the quest for equality takes place in an enlarged setting, all views, including those pertaining to equality, are fully considered. As a result, judgments are not based on a form of private reason grounded in unexamined prejudice, and thus the quest for equality, even by those who in promoting equality do not receive all they hope for, seems genuine and credible, and furthermore, the principle remains significant and vital, even if it exists outside an integrated and interrelated system of concepts.

V. SMITH'S IMPARTIAL SPECTATOR

Kant's notion of enlarged thought has been defined in terms of his rules of understanding which undergird the *sensus communis*. I have argued that these rules gain significance from the fact that in a setting where people cannot predicate their judgments on a coherent system of concepts based upon a form of pure reason, their only resort is to embrace the enlarged approach described here. But it could be claimed that while people may find Kant's rules for thinking in enlarged terms intellectually acceptable from the standpoint of the general philosophical justification, to conduct themselves in accordance with these rules, people may have to violate *essential* aspects of their nature as human beings. After all, people often enter the political arena in order to pursue matters to which they have passionate commitments. Given that the rules of enlarged thought require people to diminish the intensity of these passions so that they can engage in an enlarged discourse, it is possible that in following these rules people may act in ways that seem to violate their passions.

If one were to draw this conclusion, then the rules of understanding that have significance from the standpoint of a philosophical argument lose their significance when looked upon from the point of view of how well they may fit within peoples' natural emotional orientation. Unless this objection can be overcome, the general philosophical argument for enlarged thought will be seriously damaged. So the question becomes one of how to buttress the general argument for enlarged thought. In this section, the general argument for enlarged thought is made more complete by maintaining that Kant's rules of understanding presume a major sentiment, which would explain why citizens find it quite natural to maintain the rules of enlarged thought even if at times this means diminishing the intensity of passions. There is an important sentiment or feeling, which Adam Smith identifies, and which while not completely denying the place of passion, nonetheless works to dim the intensity of passion so that the rules of enlarged thought and what they permit, real understanding and judgment, can take place. Moreover, this major sentiment, sympathy, becomes the basis for a point of view, Smith's impartial spectator, which allows citizens who differ on a variety of questions to seek a way to accommodate their differences with the intent of achieving fairness.

In the section on sympathy in *The Theory of Moral Sentiments*, sympathy is the sentiment of "fellow feeling with any passion whatever [that others may have]."[47] As such, sympathy is predicated upon the ability of the imagination to place people into a mental position where they can understand the viewpoints of others. "By the imagination we place ourselves in his situation, we conceive ourselves enduring all the same torments, we enter as it were his body, and become in some measure the same person with him, and thence form some ideas of his sentiments, and even feel something which, though weaker in degree, is not together unlike them."[48] The immediate moral implication of a sympathetic feeling is that it encourages people to overcome the temptation to permit self-love to be the dominant emotion. Indeed, a person will "naturally prefer himself to all mankind, yet he dare not look mankind in the face, and avow that he acts according to this principle." For, as Smith says, this is a principle that "no impartial spectator can go along with"; instead, the impartial spectator requires that he "humble the arrogance of his self-love, and bring it down to something which other men can go along with."[49] Here the sentiment of sympathy provides one with the capacity to resist the temptation to think only of oneself, and this fact makes possible the impartial spectator point of view on the world, which embodies in our character the moral premise that "there can be no proper motive for hurting our neighbor, there can be no incitement to do evil to another which mankind will go along with, except just indignation for evil which that other has done to us."[50]

Smith's position does not rule out the possibility of an individual having the freedom to choose and then to pursue the life plans he defines. Society must facilitate this prospect, to be sure. But from the point of view of the impartial spectator "in the race for wealth, and honours, and preferments, he may run as hard as he can, and strain every nerve and every muscle, in order to outstrip all his competitors. But if he should justle [sic], or throw down any of them, the indulgence of the spectators is entirely at an end. It is a violation of fair play, which they [impartial spectators] cannot admit of. . . . They [impartial spectators] readily, therefore, sympathize with the natural resentment of the injured."[51]

The impartial spectator's outlook culminates in a commitment to treat others fairly, as the course of the discussion in this section makes clear. The route to fairness is communication among diverse persons, which the impartial spectator makes possible by encouraging us to reach beyond our own self to understand other selves. Indeed, the impartial spectator's point of view pushes us toward others with an empathetic intent, initially, of simply understanding them. Smith says that by consulting the "judge within," the impartial spectator, it is possible to make a "proper comparison between our own interests and those of other people."[52] But in addition, we communicate not only to understand other views and interests, but to put our views into a state of "balance" with the views of others.[53] Here the impartial spectator point of view implies another, important dimension. To reach a judgment on the best balance of interests, people must determine where they should modify their views and where they should hold fast to them. In order to achieve a balance of opinion, people must assume the viewpoint of the impartial spectator and avoid the distortions engendered by the intense passion of self-love. Smith says of the person who is not capable of this step that "his interests ["influenced by selfish and original passions of human nature"], as long as they are surveyed from his station, can never be put into the *balance with our own*, can never restrain us from doing whatever may tend to promote our own, how ruinous soever to him. Before we can make any proper comparison of those opposite interests, we must change our position. We must view them, neither from our own place nor from his, neither with our own eyes nor yet with his, but from the place and with the eyes of a third person, who has no particular connection with either, and who judges with impartiality between us."[Emphasis mine.][54]

The impartial spectator as the "third person" suggests a point of view that allows citizens to try to convince each other to modify the views they hold, as each seeks to find a way to balance the interests of the members of the society. For instance, others present me with arguments that I ponder and if I find them satisfactory, perhaps I will then modify my views. The same possibility works in their case, too. What makes it possible for me to be open to the influence of arguments that I may disagree with is that I, like others, can limit a natural tendency to think in self-serving terms by virtue of a sympathetic nature which compels human beings to not harm others.

Conceived in these terms, the sentiment of sympathy upon which the impartial spectator is built is a powerful feeling that counteracts the thrust of intense private passion and allows people to do precisely what Kant's rules of understanding encourage. Indeed, to follow the direction implied by the sentiment of the impartial spectator, people must not permit their passions to prejudice their understanding lest they be unable to create a unity and coherence among diverse views, a unity and coherence that can sustain support for a common approach to a given issue. For Smith there is a longing "for that relief which nothing can afford him [or each particular person] but the entire concord of the affections of the spectators with his own."[55]

But concord cannot be achieved if intense passions distort understanding and frustrate peoples' ability to listen and to fully consider the arguments of others who hold different views from their own. To move to harmony a person must "flatten . . . the sharpness of its [passion's] natural tone, in order to reduce it to harmony and concord with the emotions of those who are about him."[56] As in Kant, what distorts are intense feelings that prejudice outlooks and prevent people from comparing views and reaching a mutual basis for conduct. The impartial spectator's sympathy, then, "cools" the passions to the point where they do not interfere with the person's ability to make judgments that bring consensus among diversity.

As they are continually placing themselves in his situation, and thence conceiving emotions similar to what he feels; so he is as constantly placing himself in theirs, and thence conceiving some degree of that coolness about his own fortune, which he is sensible that they will view it. As they are constantly considering what they themselves would feel, if they actually were the sufferers, so he is constantly led to imagine in what manner he would be affected if he was only one of the spectators of his own situation. As their sympathy makes them look at it in some measure with his eyes, so his sympathy makes him look at it with theirs, especially when in their presence, and acting under their observation: and, as the reflected passion which he thus conceives is much weaker than the original one, it necessarily abates the violence of what he felt before he came into their presence.[57]

The impartial spectator reduces the impact and intensity of passion so that the psychological distance between people who disagree can be reduced to permit a conversation that can achieve mutual understanding and a commitment to balance interests. In this case, passions are not denied; they remain a natural part of life. But they are modified by the impartial spectator's sympathy so that they do not impede real communication, another natural and normal part of life.

Finally, in making sympathy and its moral requirement to not harm others such a central motivation in the outlooks of citizens, it is clear that the conversation of citizens makes fairness a fundamental dimension of the public life. (I build upon this view more fully in chapters 5 and 7,) This view is made manifest by the fact that for Smith when people sympathize with others they tend to sympathize with "the sorrow of our fellow-creature whenever we see his distress, so we likewise enter in his abhorrence and aversion for whatever has given occasion to it. Our heart, as it adopts and beats time to his grief, so is it likewise animated with that spirit by which he endeavors to drive away or destroy the cause of it."[58] The impartial spectator is built upon this sympathetic outlook, because from the spectator point of view each person is part of a multitude, and what afflicts one may afflict another.[59] "The compassion of the spectator must arise altogether from the consideration of what he himself would feel if he was reduced to the same unhappy situation."[60] This understanding would encourage people who look at the world from an impartial spectator view to focus upon, in their political discussions, the claims of the sufferer and to seek to include in the balance of interests that is created, a remedy for his suffering, should it be the case that upon examination the sufferer's claims are deemed to be worthy ones.

The spectator demands justice because "society cannot subsist among those who are at all times ready to hurt and injure one another."[61] Without justice, the social bonds would be destroyed, and in this case people would relate to each other from a very intense passionate commitment to self-interest, and then the impartial spectator would be destroyed. Seen against this background, Kant's enlarged discourse is sustained by a major sentiment that lies at the heart of enlarged thought itself, sympathy. It is this sentiment that buttresses Kant's faculty of judgment or his rules for common human understanding by making them appear to be natural and necessary from an emotional as well as intellectual standpoint. Indeed, without these rules and the sympathy which undergirds them, people could not participate in one of life's most essential undertakings, communication to find the basis for fairness throughout society.

VI. KANT'S *SENSUS COMMUNIS* AND SMITH'S IMPARTIAL SPECTATOR

Seen in the context of Kant's *sensus communis* and Smith's impartial spectator, the core aspect of a political culture is the understanding that derives from the effort on the part of persons to constantly reach beyond their own views and attempt to see as others see, so that each can finally make his own views less partial and more whole. If made the basis of politics, enlarged thinking can work to avert the disasters inherent in deliberations that are found in political life. Often enough political talk proceeds by excluding views that challenge existing understandings that one already holds. The tactic of political talk is to limit full consideration of diverse views and exclude some claims. This effort, when successful, creates deep social antagonisms which make force and manipulation the rule of politics.

But political judgments made on this basis necessarily hinder and distort understanding, and this fact would limit the capacity of citizens in a society to make judgments best suited to the needs of critically reflective citizens. As a result, an enlarged approach to making judgments must be entertained especially when the alternative, a system of coherent concepts based on Platonic reason, does not seem practical. In undertaking an enlarged approach the idea of respect for persons becomes a major and significant value of the culture, for without it, enlarged judgments would not be possible. In this way enlarged thinking demonstrates that respect for persons, a value of great importance to liberal societies, does in fact have significance to a liberal culture and to the critically reflective persons in that culture.

3

The Motivation
for an Enlarged Culture

I. THE NATURE OF THE CONFLICT

The general philosophical justification for enlarged thought, while demonstrating the general value of an enlarged culture, does not demonstrate why citizens in an actual liberal society would find an enlarged culture of fundamental importance to their having a strong obligation to authority. To address this issue, it is necessary to discuss the nature of the actual hopes and conflicts in a liberal society, and then to show that given both these things—hopes and conflicts—an enlarged culture becomes a matter of central importance. The basic conflict liberal citizens face is that there are competing conceptions of the way of life that liberal states should support. These differing conceptions stem from competing notions of what the concept "development of persons" or "respect for persons" means. This conflict in meanings is best characterized by making reference to a pervasive difference of opinion in liberal society concerning the best way of life people hope to see realized.

Some, as Ronald Dworkin demonstrates, argue that liberal society should be neutral among the different conceptions of life that people may hold. Here, the view of liberalism "takes as fundamental the idea that government must not take sides on moral issues, and it supports only such egalitarian measures as can be shown to result from that principle."[1] I refer to this view as the individualist strain in liberalism. An important proponent of this view, Robert Nozick, argues for a society that permits a person "the ability to regulate and guide its life in accordance with some overall conception it chooses to accept. Such

47

an overall conception, and knowing how we are doing in terms of it, is important to the kinds of goals we formulate for ourselves and the kind of beings we are."[2] In this setting a person gains "the capacity to so shape his life [so that he] can have or strive for a meaningful life."[3] To provide this opportunity, citizens are assumed to be protected by "side constraints," which are entitlements that cannot be denied, and people use them to secure their quest to attain their own self-defined notion of the good.[4] A system of government must be created to protect these side constraints, and thus Nozick advocates the need for a "dominant protective association," whose purpose is to invoke procedures that can always maintain a setting where these entitlements are secure.[5] Here the "government that claims his [a citizen's] allegiance . . . must be *neutral* between its citizens."[6] As a consequence, there are likely to be different versions of individualist views of life, and some of them may conflict with each other. In this case, government's role is to resolve the differences in a way that protects liberty and neutrality.

In arguing for side constraints to protect neutrality, Nozick suggests that there are approved rules persons must follow in pursuing their goals. Further, the resulting distribution of wealth that follows from the pursuit of one's choices is just if it arises from "legitimate means," or from the adherence to the accepted rules of the social order.[7] If some people in following the rules that secure choice accumulate more wealth than others, the resulting distribution is fair. By contrast, Nozick rejects what he refers to as "patterned distributional principles of justice," such as he finds in Rawls, because these principles deny the "right to choose what to do with what one has."[8]

The individualist view, then, does not deny that social rules exist to restrain the actions of individuals. These rules restrain persons in a direction that protects the broadest opportunities for life choices possible. In this case, it is inevitable that the state in remaining neutral among these choices permits actions to take place that have contradictory moral implications. Furthermore, it would be impossible to rule out some form of equality of distribution of basic goods, for these goods provide basic opportunities that permit individuals to act upon their own life plans. If the state failed to provide these goods to all, then some would be denied the same freedom granted to others. To repeat, as Dworkin says, equality is an acceptable value here only if it serves a neutralist commitment.[9]

In general, on the individualist view, a government treats its citizens with equal dignity and respect by providing to each person the protections and benefits one needs in order to have the freedom to both define and to pursue that form of life one determines is best for oneself. But the notion of treating persons with respect and dignity may be interpreted in another way too, and in the second way, the state acts on behalf of a commitment to a notion of a moral right, which it attempts to make the fundamental basis of society, and it hopes to secure equal respect by helping citizens to embody this idea of right into their own lives. I call this version of liberalism the communalist strain because it is based upon the understanding that society should, to use Rawls's words, reflect a commitment to general and comprehensive moral doctrines. These doctrines are general "in that they apply to a wide range of subjects, and comprehensive in that they include conceptions of what is of value in human life, ideals or personal virtue and character that are to inform our thought and conduct as a whole."[10]

Thus, in one version of the communalist view, based on a communal view of equality favored by Dworkin,[11] the objective of government is to treat "its citizens as equals, and [this view of liberalism] insists on moral neutrality only to the degree that equality requires it."[12] The state must not impose on a citizen anything that he could not accept "without abandoning his sense of his equal worth."[13] To treat people as equals means that "each be permitted to use for the projects to which he devotes his life, no more than an equal share of the resources available for all."[14] In this view, the society is a community providing certain shared goods, and citizens in the society must share in these goods equally.[15] These goods enable people to regard the society "as their community," and they permit citizens to think of the future as in some sense "their future."[16]

Dworkin's version of communalism is predicated on a particular conception of persons as members of a community willing to shape their lives so that they live in accordance with the principle that no one can have "more than an equal share of the resources available to all." To think in these terms is to allow a particular conception of character, in this case one that values equality of resource distribution, "inform" the outlooks and choices that people make in life. Indeed, unlike the individualist, who would reject any such doctrine unless it could support neutrality, the communalist sees certain doctrines as necessary guides that should shape the character of people and limit their life choices in ways that are in keeping with the intent of the moral doctrine. Only then can real dignity and freedom be realized. In this case, the state is not neutral, and it cannot be if the comprehensive moral doctrine is to be realized.

Other people define the meaning of their communalist view in terms of a different general and comprehensive moral doctrine. It is not that these people always or even necessarily must reject equality as Dworkin understands it; it is only that they wish to emphasize the centrality of those virtues that their particular conception of community makes important. In this regard, some see a republican tradition in American politics in which individual interests are subordinate to the classical civic ideals of "unity, harmony and the public good."[17] John Patrick Diggins argues that whereas the Federalists were attracted by the notion that virtue should limit the activities of citizens, practically they knew that men were motivated by self-interest. Getting citizens to accord their lives to a public good could be achieved only if the constitution erected a form of mixed government that could place interest against interest and thus create a balance more conducive to public order. For people like John Adams "mixed government could not be made by virtue but . . . virtue could flow from it."[18]

But for the modern republican, resort to government mechanisms that balance interests is not sufficient to secure civic virtue. Citizens must also learn to think in terms that replicate the experience of a civic republican point of view in which each works consciously for the good of the society. William Sullivan hopes to recover this tradition in the American setting by restoring its central symbols of "citizen and commonwealth—the moral imperative to live according to the principles of justice and mutual support grounded in civil covenant."[19] To achieve justice, citizens must learn to view society in classical terms as an integrated whole, which is based on a common telos or end.[20] In this view, each of the various capacities of human beings are integrated into a system that is a "developing whole."[21] Society is not seen, as in the individualist view, with each individual acting as an instrument to individual ends, but instead, in this organic view, initiated by Aristotle but found in its modern form in Hegel, Marx, Durkheim, Dewey, and Parsons,[22] each individual contributes to the good of the whole, and in doing so, finds fellowship and justice.[23] Justice in this case means that each is part of the whole, and thus each participates in a "proportionate sharing of the common good."[24] As in the writings of Alasdair MacIntyre, individuals are a part of traditions for constituting a life of virtue, and in carrying out one's life in keeping with these traditions, one is able to realize one's true ends.[25]

None of this is meant to diminish the importance of the constitutional process in the civic republican point of view. The constitution establishes a basic framework by which all must abide in pursuing their goals in the political system. Indeed, the constitutional process would make possible a form of what Sullivan calls "uncoerced civic participation" in the forming of the common good.[26] In this view there are authoritative political institutions which make and enforce the law that all citizens and public officials are subject to. In the contemporary setting (and this part of the politics of republicanism is not developed by Sullivan), policies are made and enforced by and through adherence to a constitutional process that establishes the supreme law of the land for all citizens to follow. Citizens fear the corruption of politics, says Sullivan, from self-interest concerns.[27] To thwart corruption, public officials and citizens are to conduct themselves in the manner suggested by their constitution. As they do, citizens gain respect and public honor. Indeed, as Sullivan says, people gain rewards and offices on the basis of "advancement of this vision of the common good."[28] This means that public officials win respect and honor when their actions preserve a tradition of the search for the common good in politics, and ordinary citizens are allowed to enhance their personal welfare when their efforts are shown to contribute to the politics of the public good too. Not only must citizens uphold the constitutional process, but they must adhere to the results of the process as well. To act against this objective is to demonstrate a lack of respect for public or civic virtue. In making this claim, however, it becomes clear that even constitutionalism survives only when citizens have a commitment to maintain civic virtues that symbolize the fact that the "final concern of politics, like that of the family though in a more universal way, is mutual moral cultivation."[29] The thrust of moral virtue is the teaching that the authentic growth and development of the self is a mutual concern of others, and public life, in its quest for the common good, is designed to realize this concern.[30]

As in MacIntyre, the most important part of the shared traditions are the virtues the traditions cultivate. Yet MacIntyre, like Sullivan, sees the modern who acts in keeping with the canons of individualist liberalism as viewing virtue as an impediment to freedom. If the modern chooses to substitute his own meaning for traditional virtues like honor and desert, this may be understood for him, depending on the circumstances, as a symbol of his independence from those value contexts that deny freedom. "Hence [in the modern world] notions of desert and honour become detached from the context in which they were originally at home," and as a result, they are no longer the shaping influences they should be.[31] As shaping influences, virtues like honor and desert are supposed to mean that people are to use their talents and skills to promote the public good and the general welfare of all. Virtuous people contribute to making possible a setting where each person both contributes to other individuals in particular and to the good of the whole in general. This understanding is the basis for a society based on reciprocity in which people are constantly committed to contribute to one another's lives in ways that are essential to protecting the common good that all share. Instead, in the individualist setting, these virtues are redefined to mean that what is best for oneself is the most important goal in life, and the general welfare can be given a secondary importance.

In practical terms, then, the commitment to virtue means that real fellowship among citizens presumes a chance to achieve reciprocity, but reciprocity itself "has no meaning without a conception of what the good polity should be like, of what each citizen requires to share the good life of virtue."[32] If this is so, then a politics based on a shared commitment to civic virtue and the quest to found society upon a common good requires that citizens actually succeed in defining a common good in each of the various issue domains that contribute to reciprocity among citizens. If that common good cannot be defined for basic issues like welfare, agriculture, defense, and so on, then the goal of the civic republican of basing politics on a set of common understandings that each can contribute to is threatened. Thus, in the absence of a firmly held common good, reciprocity is a distant goal even for a society committed to attain it. Society must learn to tolerate the absence of a perfected reciprocal scheme, as citizens continue to search for a way to attain reciprocity in a fuller form. That is precisely the problem the modern liberal citizen faces as he tries to accommodate a broad range of diverse needs in a social setting committed to achieve mutual cooperation within an enlarged culture. As we argue in the next section, owing to the commitment to achieve basic rights and liberties for the sake of the development of persons, there will be diverse life plans, often posing morally contradictory ways of life, and in a society committed to respect for diversity and cooperation, the search for a common good must always give way to less than perfect results.

From the preceding, it is clear that communalists articulate their views of the correct comprehensive moral doctrine differently from each other. Some emphasize a need for distributing basic goods on an equal basis, while others emphasize the need for teaching people virtue as a basis either for the politics of a common good or for achieving a life lived to its "true" ends. And even if some communalists emphasize elements of each of the points of view found in different communalist arguments and thus differ from those versions that do not, still, communalists share the commitment to teach to all citizens a comprehensive moral doctrine. And in this they differ from liberal individualists. What for the communalist is the moral basis for a dignified life is for the individualist a "hindrance" to freedom. And this perception undermines, from the communalist standpoint, the chances for real freedom.[33]

II. THE CRITICALLY REFLECTIVE CITIZEN AND AN ENLARGED CULTURE

There are practical implications of these different orientations for how citizens discuss issues. Since citizens start from one or the other strain in making judgments of actual political questions that affect society, it is inevitable that society will be characterized by a debate that reflects these different views. Further, it should be clear that since there are diverse variants of individualist and communalist views, it is the case that differences between holders of each view will extend to differing forms of individualism clashing with each other and different forms of communalism clashing with each other.[34]

But despite these differences of view it should not be overlooked that liberal citizens (and here I have in mind ideal liberal citizens) who support different strains recognize that they are citizens of a liberal culture, and thus each finds the liberal character of the regime to be a desirable quality. Moreover, ideal liberal citizens hope to be a part of a culture that makes it possible for them to be critically reflective persons. As such, liberal citizens want to be in a position to make judgments about public policy that have impact on shaping the actual policies and laws of the society. The ideal liberal citizen hopes that the effect of his critically evaluative dimension will be a society that makes more likely the prospect of self-respect for all citizens.

While it is true that even as critically reflective persons, liberal citizens no doubt might privately support one strain more than another; still, liberal citizens know that in their public conduct they must resist the temptation to create a world that eliminates one strain in favor of the other. The reason for this view is that liberal citizens are in the main principled realists. As admirers of the regime's liberal character, they are committed to uphold the principle of protecting basic rights and liberties for all in order to secure the development and self-respect of all persons. But they know that the tension between the two strains is ongoing and that to push for the elimination of one strain in the name of the other would culminate in undermining this principle. Indeed, there seem to be two dangerous consequences of the extreme view. In the first instance, a dominant strain would make it impossible for holders of the other strain to achieve the way of life they sought, and for these people rights and liberties would, because they could not help to secure self-development, lose their significance. The second consequence of an extreme view, or what I refer to as crude extremism, is to undermine the authentic expression of the dominant strain, with the result that rights not only lose their significance, but they are completely denied. Examples of each instance follow.

Take an example of the first instance, where rights and liberties lose their significance. An extreme communalist committed to make traditional religion a common basis for each person's life might argue that in order to achieve this goal, it would be necessary to deny atheists a chance to publicize their beliefs. Perhaps atheists could practice their beliefs in private, but if they were to discuss them with nonatheists, they might be charged with violating the law. Since the way of life atheists prize would include this type of discussion, the communalist's moral position would keep atheists from easily pursuing the way of life they found desirable. Atheists could be granted the same rights and liberties provided to others, just as long as they did not use them to promote atheism. They might even be permitted to use their freedom of speech and participation to try to change the law to allow all views pertaining to atheism to be aired; but as long as the extreme communalist had his way and the law pertaining to atheism remained in force, atheists would be forbidden from trying to convince others of the virtues of the atheist position. The atheists would no doubt believe that their rights had little significance, because they could not use their rights and liberties to have others consider carefully and seriously a way of life that they value.

Or an extreme individualist might seek to establish a regime with laws against discussing limitations on wealth accumulation. Again, because he lived in a liberal society, he might support providing people the same basic rights and liberties. Citizens for wealth limitations might use their rights to argue for ending the ban on discussing wealth limitations. But if the extreme individualist had his way, then this ban would not be lifted. As in the preceding case, individuals for limitations might think that their rights had lost their significance because the rights and liberties could not be used to discuss an important and highly valued way of life, a way of life that, even if not accepted by others, was at least well understood by others.

As I argued in the first chapter, the liberal citizen is always ready to critique the state's use of rights and liberties on the basis of how well they contribute to the development of persons. If a person thinks that the state's policies undermine the view of individualism or communalism he adheres to, he is ready to protest these policies. In this case, the protesters explain that the state may protect basic rights and liberties. But because it fails to allow the way of life one most respects, the basic rights and liberties are not being used to sustain the development of *all* persons, and in consequence (from the standpoint of the protester at least), the basic rights and liberties lose their significance. The critically reflective person hopes to avoid committing the same mistake by resisting the temptation to formulate his judgments in extreme individualist or communalist terms. Otherwise, he understands that his actions might have the same effect of making rights and liberties lose their significance for many people who would be unable by virtue of extremist judgments and actions to pursue their development.

Extreme versions of either strain are avoided for another reason, too. Extreme versions manifested in their crude form lead to actions that undermine the authentic expression of the dominating strain and also as a consequence deny rights and liberties to a large part of the citizenry. Thus, a crude form of communalism may require that to achieve a society based on respect for traditional virtues, in the manner of MacIntyre, it is necessary to establish the power of a religious authority to impose virtue. Given the resistance to this project likely to arise from modern individualists, the state might then have to resort to tactics which require the officials to resist and overcome opposition to its policies. To do so, the officials may manifest forms of conduct that violate virtues like honesty and honor or they may even undermine the policies of the common good, as demanded by the republican tradition. For instance, to secure the moral foundation of the regime as the crude communalist understands that foundation, it might be necessary for the latter to appear to be subservient to both the law and to the constitutional process when discussing matters before the public, but in fact the crude communalist might accept actions which violate the law in order to suppress those who threaten the state's attempt to instill respect for virtue. The state, in acting in this manner, no longer feels that the common good, as defined by the legitimate processes of constitutional government, protects the moral foundation of social life, and so it would argue that it must act independently of the constitution, even if in doing so it defies the constitution and the laws promulgated under the constitution. Public officials would see a virtue in lying and deception, and they would define as honorable any violation of the law that preserves morality (as the crude communalist understands morality). Further, the state would no doubt outlaw any consideration of points of view which oppose the state's position. In this case, atheism would not just be banned, but citizens would not even be provided the liberty to openly criticize the ban on the discussion of atheism.

Similarly, an individualist life-style which was pushed to its most crude form would undermine its authentic nature by according to some the right of unlimited individualism. These "super" individuals would stand as role models for the rest, and to protect their place in society, it would be necessary to arrange the social and political context so that others would have to deny their own hopes and aspirations for the sake of supporting the life-styles of the "super" individuals. Here, a form of individualist life-style would emerge which actually denied most individuals a chance for self-development. Furthermore, as in the crude communalist case, it is likely that the crude individualist would resist opposition by banning all efforts to put limits on wealth accumulation of the "super" individuals, and this policy would extend to banning all discussion of wealth limitations as well as denying all citizens the right to even challenge the state's decision to continue the ban. In either case, crude communalism or crude individualism, citizens would no longer be guaranteed the right to challenge the state's authority and to demand that it change its authoritarian manner. Then it would not just be the case that rights lacked significance, as in the first example of extremism, but that rights had to be completely denied.

Critically reflective citizens have much to fear from the imposition of an extreme form of communalism or individualism, then. In this setting, there would be the fear that in addition to the loss of rights, the critically reflective form of life itself would not be tolerated. Since the whole demeanor of the critically reflective citizen resists the imposition in the extreme of even the view he supports, this attitude would be considered dangerous by a state committed to either extreme communalism or individualism. Critically reflective citizens see grounds for their fears in what they perceive as tendencies toward extremism that exist already. Thus in the present society there is a recurrent fear that certain self-appointed "moral exemplars" will arise from religious spheres, win support, and impose the "right" way of life onto everyone, thus denying provision of basic rights to all as well as a critically reflective life form. In the same way, the individualist dimension in its extreme form is manifested in the tendency to celebrate those with great wealth who gain their wealth not through contributing to production, but through the manipulation of the stock market. The current fear for many is that if left unrestrained, these people threaten the material foundations of the productive order because they manage to extract from the productive process resources that they simply use for their own benefit, and do not reinvest these resources in improving the economic base so that there will be greater opportunities for the development of ever larger numbers of persons. In this situation, only a few could prosper, and to protect the few against the rest, basic rights as well as the critically reflective life form would have to be denied the less fortunate.

Given these concerns, the critically reflective citizen expects to prevent the emergence of a perfectionist concept of the good society that embodies either strain in the extreme sense. An alternative vision emerges, and this is the hope for an approach to issues that constantly seeks a way to accommodate the different strains in order to maintain each in a way that is as close as possible to each strain's most authentic rendering. What sustains this possibility is an enlarged culture.

In an enlarged culture, citizens must presume that their own understandings are limited and that to be made more whole, they must contrast and test their own views against those held by others. Thus a communalist-oriented person recognizes that the judgments he makes are incomplete if they are not tested against opposing forms of communalist and individualist views. A similar position is taken by the individualist-oriented person. In the process of testing views in this manner, citizens search for an agreement all can accept, but they know that, owing to the continued existence of each strain in society, there is a good chance that any agreement will be subject to further debate, a point I discuss more completely at the conclusion of chapter 5. This means that citizens will do the best they can to narrow their differences and to "balance" their interests, as Smith says, but still, after a policy is established, it is likely that some will still disagree with it, and these people will continue to try to convince others to work with them to change it.

The last point should be understood against the context of the fact that a liberal society accepts and makes preeminent a commitment to constitutional government and thereby provides a fixed procedure for determining policy outcomes. The process has a formal element, defined in terms of the procedural rules that must be followed if the results of the process are to be considered binding. The typical formal rule used in this process is the rule that a majority vote is generally binding, especially in legislative settings. Reflected here is a strong desire, emanating perhaps from the republican tradition, for achieving a common good or goods in the various policy areas. But because there are diverse understandings of the common good, and because the commitment to protect rights and liberties for the development of persons protects these different understandings and allows them to be expressed in the political process, the results of this process are often seen as falling short of the hope of achieving a common good. Citizens are constantly asked and indeed exhorted to find a way to accommodate their differences and to accept a policy that does not perfectly achieve what each might hope for. The outcome is not a common good but a policy which some support more than others, and the people who do not find themselves in wholehearted agreement may then go on to attempt to change the policy society has adopted by influencing the state and the public to reconsider the policy. Even if the commitment to constitutional government and the rule of law is maintained, this dual commitment does not make possible the communalist hope for a firmly entrenched public good or goods existing at the heart of the social and political life.

The question at this point is whether people who disagree with the policy outcome will still support the decision process in a strong sense even when they do not agree with the results it produces. The possibility of citizen disenchantment is avoided where the decision process is located within (and, as I argue in the next section and in chapter 5, made instrumental to) an enlarged culture. In this case, the decision process symbolizes a full discussion of the issues, where all the known, different views are seriously considered as people search for the best accommodation. For instance, where atheism or questions of wealth limitations are known positions, as in our society, then people who disagree with these views but who have an enlarged mind must test their own views against these positions as well as others that exist. This means that atheism must not just be discussed in terms of whether or not to discuss it, but atheism must be a part of the discussion of religious freedom, and atheists can expect to have their views made a part of the public debate on religion and the accommodation that the public policy process achieves. Similarly, on the issue of wealth limitations, citizens in an enlarged culture must not just have a right to argue for a chance to discuss this idea, but they must have in fact a chance to promote it and to have it be part of the balance that results. In each instance, citizens would not always win the position they supported in the precise way they had hoped, but they would still have a chance to use their rights to promote the view of persons they held, and thus an enlarged culture would secure for these rights real significance.

As a consequence of locating the decision process in an enlarged discourse, this process gains respect from citizens, even when citizens do not always win the results they may hope for. Citizens can accept and respect the results of a process even when they disagree with them because the decision process is built upon an enlarged discourse that, on the whole, ensures that each strain survives in a manner which is in keeping with its basic nature and intent. Citizens know without an enlarged discourse what would result is a setting where one strain or the other emerged in extreme form, not only denying the essential character of the strain it was attempting to realize, but threatening as well a setting which protects rights and liberties for all. If the formal decision process yielded this outcome, citizens would lose respect for it, and they would not have a strong sense of obligation to the state that maintained it.

For the reasons just presented, then, there is a practical motivation to make an enlarged culture a central benefit of a liberal society. The hopes of critically reflective liberal citizens for a society where rights and liberties promote the development of persons ultimately rest on whether or not an enlarged culture can be realized.

III. WILLIAM GALSTON'S LIBERALISM

In developing the practical importance of the enlarged culture to a liberal society, some might argue that the liberal state provides more things than just this; in particular, it provides the rule of law, diversity, social peace, absence of extreme poverty, and so on, and if it does, why are not these things either separately or taken together a more important basis for a strong obligation than an enlarged culture? The answer to this question is that aspects like those just mentioned are important in a liberal regime only because they are conceived in such a way that they help to contribute to an enlarged culture. In effect, rights and liberties, the rule of law and some of the other elements just mentioned gain their overall importance to a liberal society because they are located in and in some cases are even instrumental to an enlarged culture. This argument can best be made by reference to William Galston's work.

Liberalism for Galston is not an empty formalism that is based simply on protecting certain public procedures that all must follow in resolving issue differences. Instead, liberalism contains a commitment to a minimalist notion of the good; in particular, that liberal societies "are, on balance, most conducive to individual development."[35] But stipulating what a liberal regime remains committed to provide, in this case, a setting that makes the development of all persons possible, does not by itself help to specify the full substantive nature of the liberal culture. And the reason for this is that the individualist/communalist dichotomy always manifests itself in such a way as to make the definition of a substantive culture that secures the development of persons difficult to attain. This fact can be seen in Galston's view of liberal culture as well.

Galston argues that "liberal societies believe that individuals are, at least in part, responsible for the use they make of opportunities for development and that individuals are entitled to make claims on resources based on what they have achieved. Liberal societies claim to be more just than those societies that deny the moral force of claims based upon achievement, as well as those societies that ignore claims based upon need."[36] Implicit in this view of development is the conflict between the individualist and communalist strains. The notion of providing rewards to persons based on achievement is an individualist conception of persons, which may conflict with the notion of distribution based on need. The merit conception makes as a priority the development and the flourishing of individual talents and abilities. But in providing to all based on a conception of generic needs, then individuals understand society as a community, which affords goods to people not solely on the basis of merit, but simply on the basis of a fundamental and shared concept of need. And the notion of need may at times require that individual rewards for merit be limited so that basic needs can be secured for all.

I have made much of this tension, and unlike Galston, I have argued that it is basic to understanding the substantive nature of a liberal culture. Given the fact that there exists a conflict between the way the "development of persons" is to be construed, and given as well that each strain is necessarily for its own good limited by the other, then what facilitates an accommodation is at the heart of substantive liberal culture. And that dimension is an enlarged culture.

This understanding is crucial to conceptualizing the nature of the basic elements of a liberal culture which Galston discusses. Galston says that minimally a liberal state must provide social peace or the "amelioration of conflict"; the rule of law or a "framework of reasonably stable expectations conducive to the planned pursuit of individual purposes"; recognition of diversity or respect "for diversity of tastes, talents and life-plans"; a tendency toward inclusiveness of all under the protection of that law; minimum decency or elimination of "wanton brutality" and "desperate poverty"; scope for development or full support of the "development of individual talents and capacities"; a form of distributive justice that satisfies need-based claims "stemming from the simple fact of individual existence," and desert-based claims arising from differences of individual endeavor and contribution; openness or "unfettered pursuit and promulgation of truth"; and respect for privacy.[37]

Of course, these are important elements in a liberal culture; indeed, they may be important to any regime, liberal or not, that seeks to provide justice to its citizens. But in a liberal culture where the individualist/communalist tension is prevalent, how are these elements to be understood? For instance, an individualist discussing the rule of law may argue that the latter must permit individuals a chance to pursue their own tastes by banning public prayer in all public places. Others may understand the rule of law as protecting the community's view of what constitutes the basis of moral standards, respect for religious authority, and thus the rule of law protects religious symbols and prayer for all religions in public places. Here religious freedom under the rule of law means not freedom *from* but freedom *for* religion.

Or take the notion of openness and the commitment to truth. In discussing the facts of social welfare programs, the government must state the facts truthfully. How many people have taken advantage of the program, how many more need the program, how much has it cost, and how much will it cost to include those still standing in line for welfare? But that presentation of the facts will always be affected by the point of view one takes on social welfare programs. From the individualist view, one can argue that the number of people still waiting in line for the program, as well as the number of people still in the program, signify that people have lost their initiative as a result of this program. From the communalist view, it is different. Many people have been helped, and as a result a good number have left, but much still needs to be done to help the rest. In this example, the essential elements of a liberal society that Galston identifies, the need to balance need-based claims with desert-based ones, are in conflict. This conflict once again reflects the tension in a liberal society between individualist and communalist based claims, and to work to resolve them means that it is necessary to work within an accommodationist view. As in the first example of the rule of law, each side realizes that it will have to modify its view in light of the others. As a result of a formal decision process, the discussion will continue even after a decision is reached, because many people will still not be totally convinced that the accommodation arrived at is the best solution. A better one may be possible.

But what makes this kind of discourse possible is an enlarged culture. In maintaining it, the society maintains an accommodationist approach to issues like those just discussed. But to protect this discourse setting, it is necessary to provide Galston's basic elements in a way that will at least assure an enlarged culture. In this way, Galston's elements are viewed as instrumental to a higher end. For instance, a conception of the rule of law that threatened this discourse would threaten the liberal order. In chapters 5, 6, and 8, the argument is designed to demonstrate, at least in part, the nature that Galston's basic elements must have if the enlarged setting is to be secured. Once this discourse is protected, then arguments can continue about the "better" or "best" way to conceptualize these elements, but this argument cannot take place unless there is an agreement in society concerning how these elements should be understood to make possible an enlarged culture.

Finally, the enlarged culture gains further importance as a central benefit because in making possible an accommodation between the individualist and communalist strains, it supports as well a central and major good of a liberal society, a respect for diversity. In the view presented here, then, diversity as a central element of a liberal society that Galston identifies is not so much instrumental to an enlarged culture as it is a central benefit of an enlarged culture, a benefit that citizens in a liberal regime prize very highly. As a result, the rule of law and the other elements Galston values, insofar as they support an enlarged culture, support as well what an enlarged culture secures, a respect for and a tolerance of diversity.

The enlarged culture supports diversity in two ways. First, it contributes to a cooperative setting for society. A liberal society as we argue in the next chapter and in chapter 7, must maintain a setting where the different roles can be arranged to facilitate different life plans, defined in either communalist or individualist terms. For this to happen, people must see others as potential contributors to a cooperative arrangement that each is willing to contribute to by shouldering the necessary burdens and sacrifices.[38] But unless citizens can understand how the various members contribute to each other, then it is likely that people will be less prone to see others as potential contributors, and this perception will threaten the cooperative ethos of the society. But where people have an enlarged understanding of the way the society works, the psychological distance between people is reduced, there is a greater likelihood that citizens can understand the diverse contributions of the members, and finally, as a result, society is more capable of being the cooperative setting it must be to secure diversity.

Moreover, the practice of enlarged thinking protects diversity by combatting those experiences that threaten it. Of great importance here is that often in liberal societies, as argued in chapter 8, there are recurrences of experiences like sexual, religious, racial, and regional bigotry that lie just beneath the surface of liberal culture's apparent civility, and when bigotry rages, respect for diversity is defeated. But in a society with a strong enlarged culture, bigotry is defeated and respect for diversity triumphs.

4

A Question of Conscience

I. INTRODUCTION TO THE PROBLEM
OF THIS CHAPTER

In this chapter, the main issue concerns how people of conscience should respond to the liberal state when the latter denies a position which a person of conscience holds on a given issue. If the person has a strong obligation, he will choose civil forms of protest, and if the person has a weak obligation to authority, the person will choose noncivil forms. So the question of how a person of conscience should act when the state denies a position held by that person centers upon when that person should hold a strong obligation to the state. The answer I provide is that when the state manifests a commitment to an enlarged culture, then one is obligated in a strong sense to the state and as a result one should only manifest civil forms of protest.

II. THE PARTICULAR DILEMMA

In choosing noncivil forms of protest, a protester, as we indicated in chapter 1, seeks to change the state's policies by threatening its authority. By contrast, a person with a strong obligation uses civil forms, which seek to win changes in policy while demonstrating respect for the state.

The main argument that might be used to challenge the justifiability of noncivil forms of protest is made by Hannah Pitkin, who claims that legitimate authority is "precisely that which *ought* to be obeyed, to which one ought to consent, which deserves obedience and consent, to which rational men considering all relevant facts and issues would consent, to which consent can be justified."[1] Thus to the question why are we obliged, Pitkin's answer is that a government whose character is basically legitimate is one to which we owe an obligation. In effect, then, people are obligated to obey a legitimate regime because that is what legitimate authority means.[2] She says, "You cannot, without further elaborate explanation, maintain simultaneously *both* that this government has legitimate authority and you *and* that you have no obligation to obey it."[3] In this view, if the state is legitimate and if owing to my convictions I disagree with a particular policy, I may protest this policy but only in a way that manifests respect for the state's authority.

Still, the state's legitimacy is itself the occasion for my dilemma. A liberal state is legitimate because it supports basic rights and liberties for the purpose of securing the development of all persons. But what if the liberal state makes a policy that violates a particular position that I support from conscience? Here the state requires me to act as *it* determines, thus forcing me to violate my conscience. Why am I required to pursue civil forms of protest when the state appears to act in ways that contradict certain of its basic principles? In other terms, why should I continue to have a strong obligation to a *legitimate* state when that state makes a policy that violates my conscience and by doing so appears, at least from my point of view, to threaten my freedom of conscience?

In defense of a weak obligation in this circumstance, I could argue that because the state is legitimate, it must *always* abide by the principles that make it legitimate or I do not have to show respect for its authority when I protest its policies. In this case I am willing to undertake noncivil forms of protest, and in doing so I am even willing to risk further erosion of the basic liberties (for as we demonstrated in chapter 1, the state may respond to citizens who threaten its authority with actions that threaten the liberal character of the state). But I can rationalize the risk as justified, because in taking it I may be stopping what I see is an even graver danger, and my action may lead to a correction of state policies and thus restore a full commitment on its part to protect basic rights and liberties for all, including, in this case, full freedom of conscience.

There is a counterargument to this position that I should consider, too. It could be argued, in part as a way to further elaborate Pitkin's argument, that the question of when a legitimate state acts legitimately is a difficult issue that is clouded by the fact that a legitimate state in protecting basic rights and liberties to secure the development of persons may arrange these rights and liberties in a fashion that many may not find acceptable. Liberal states must make decisions of this sort, and when they do, they may make many unhappy owing to the fact that the ordering the state selects is not the ordering many people want. Thus at times even legitimate states must ask people to place a lesser importance on certain liberties in order to preserve other ones. In this case, it is possible that a policy I find morally objectionable has been made by the majority rule process, and the state officials, who are bound by the majority process, must give lesser weight to the claims of my conscience. Here the policy makers assert that in arranging the liberties in order of importance, they are not denying any single liberty at all. Instead, they are trying to balance the liberties in a manner that can best preserve all of them.

But have they succeeded? Thus, I am entitled to examine the justification given for the arrangement of liberties, and then I must determine whether the justification supports a strong or a weak obligation. As I proceed along these lines, it is clear that I can best sustain the life of conscience in a society that is a cooperative arrangement. In a cooperative setting, others agree to uphold the various sacrifices and burdens that are deemed necessary in order to protect major benefits like conscience. The fact is that activities based on conscience are not sustainable where others lack a willingness to tolerate those people who, in the name of conscience, raise issues, question authority, and undertake various forms of protest to government decisions. But where people accept the importance of conscience, they accept the need to endure and even to consider seriously frequent criticisms of state policy as well as public displays of protest. Unless people observed these practices, then acts of conscience would be meaningless, since there would be no audience that existed to be changed or influenced by them. A further practice that sustains acts of conscience is a government structure that is capable of being influenced by a public which is aroused by acts of conscience. Assuming my act of conscience does convince the public of my stand, for my act to be effective the state officials must be open to considering the public response. If they are, then there is a good chance my acts of conscience could change public policy in a direction that I desire. All of these roles and role expectations are critical to maintaining the life of conscience as an effective activity. In maintaining these roles, a cooperative practice is supported that succeeds in protecting conscience. And clearly what contributes to the possibility of society as a cooperative setting, not just in matters pertaining to conscience but in other matters as well, is an enlarged culture. For, as I argue in chapter 7, the experience of an enlarged culture helps to reduce the psychological distance among people. Because of this state of affairs, citizens expect that each member defines his relationship to others in terms of the need to preserve the roles and role expectations that sustain the cooperative character of the society.

In effect, if I conclude that the arrangement of liberties is acceptable, it is because overall the state has helped to create an enlarged relationship toward its citizens so that society can be a cooperative setting that facilitates the diverse needs and views of self-development, including freedom of conscience. If I were to say in the face of the state's commitment to an enlarged culture that I am right to create a noncivil form of resistance that could threaten the state and make it resort to actions which undermine its liberal character, I would be acting not from conscience but from unreasonableness, and I would undermine a state that deserves a strong obligation from me because it has used its legitimate institutions to sustain an enlarged culture. In effect, my actions would damage the enlarged culture that is the foundation of the cooperative setting upon which freedom of conscience itself rests.

Starting with the next chapter, I discuss the character a liberal state must have in order to maintain an enlarged quality toward its citizens. By doing so, the state hopes to promote within the society an enlarged culture that can facilitate a cooperative setting among the citizens. Before moving to this task, I wish to discuss another dimension of the question raised in this section concerning whether a state can deny the demands of persons based on conscience and still be owed a strong obligation.

III. CONSCIENCE AND ENLARGED THINKING

If I have succeeded in demonstrating the characteristics under which civil forms of protest are justified, it is because I have placed a high priority on cooperation. I have said that the state is owed a strong obligation if it denies a position of a person of conscience as long as it sustains an enlarged culture, for the latter contributes to a cooperative setting. But some might take the view that conscience is a preeminent value, and that when the state denies a position taken by a person of conscience, the state is unjustly repressive. As a result, citizens are always justified in holding a weak obligation when the state violates their conscience. But there is another argument that can be made to support a strong obligation to the state in this case. Once again, the state is owed a strong obligation if it secures an enlarged culture, and this time the reason is that this culture is in a liberal society *an important* authoritative ground for conscience.

For Philip Abbott "the recognition of duty is based on an autonomous decision to do what is right," but decisions of political authority make the recognition of duty, even for a state that operates by majority rule in a liberal regime, "subsequent to state determination of what is right."[4] This argument suggests that to act from a sense of duty located in moral judgment and conscience is to act from moral knowledge of what one's duties are in a given situation. But because the state may bar actions of people who make their sense of personal duty primary, then the state acts against the possibility of a life which is based on conscience and moral judgment. Abbott sees this as a major problem for liberal states, and thus he says that in a liberal state "the doctrine of conscience is only to be respected to the extent to which one's conscience supports . . . existing political authority. . . . The axe of political authority falls on conscience."[5] Here to act as conscience and moral judgment require and as the the state's political authority demands are inconsistent categories.

Principally this means that whereas the liberal state may excuse its dissenters from participating in policies which violate their conscience, it still disregards their arguments in determining policy, and the state "goes on to resolve the moral dispute according to its own determination."[6] The state interferes with individuals and even implies the view that it, rather than the individual, should be the locus of a person's moral outlook, while the state acts as a moral superior. "When one exercises moral judgment and comes to a conscientious decision in dissent from the majority, the government now, in the name of the represented (or worse, in the name of its moral expertise), asserts in effect its moral infallibility by refusing to respect the claims of the conscientious agent."[7]

Because Abbott feels that the state denies the autonomy and the authority even of individual moral judgment, the state undermines the prospects of freedom of conscience in any significant sense. As a consequence, this is one major reason why there is no morally binding justification for citizens to have a sense of obligation to the liberal state. To quote Abbott at the conclusion of his study of political obligation, "Our wrecking operation now appears to be complete. A serious attention to moral judgment forbids a moral theory of political obligation."[8]

My contention is that the state may well deny particular citizen claims of duty and not be said to undermine the significance of conscience and as a result may still be worthy of a strong obligation. This view stems from an understanding of what gives authority to conscience in the first place. The knowledge supplied by conscience has the character of moral truth by virtue of the authority that legitimizes conscience. It is presumed that all societies have traditions that perform this authorizing role. The usual sources of conscience in contemporary liberal cultures contain references to the Bible or the word of God, natural law, and even the Kantian categorical imperative. An additional important authorizing dimension of conscience, especially for liberal regimes, is deliberation.

Indeed, deliberation plays a major role in authorizing conscience in Abbott. In defining the basis for moral right, a person must (1) "demonstrate [his] act is a result of individual moral judgment," (2) "show that the basis of the decision included reference to a moral principle, the influence of relevant authorities or even in some cases a style or pattern of life," (3) "demonstrate that he has considered the consequences of his actions, both moral and nonmoral, direct and indirect" (4) "advocate that others commit themselves to a process of moral judgment described in (1)" and (5) "state a willingness to define his position in (2) and (3) and to reconsider them on the basis of new information and arguments."[9]

Persons are morally serious agents who define their own moral positions through a deliberation with others in which one attempts to convince others of the rightness of their reasons for acting as they plan to do [Abbott's conditions (4) and (5)]. In this setting, one is open to being convinced by others that one's position should be modified. It is clear that people, as they deliberate, seek to test their views against the views of others. The moral positions that emerge are legitimate only if they have been formed in this type of serious, deliberative environment. Where moral views have derived from a shared emotional experience, which has prevented people from achieving a proper reflective "distancing" to their experience so that they could deliberate with others about the right course, then people would not be basing their views on an authoritative ground, and thus conscience would not be the justification for action.

Owing to this dependency upon deliberation, it is wrong as Abbott says to presume that conscience and moral judgments manifest an arrogance in which the beliefs of others are pushed aside and discarded.[10] Abbott's "conscience talk" does consider other views, and the only problem here is determining how far one can consider others and still say the decision or moral judgment comes from the person making it. Still Abbott is confident that "we can with reasonable assurance find that point, a point which, of course, includes some consultation with and consideration of others."[11]

Moreover, since an important ground of conscience is deliberation with others, it is quite possible that on many issues, honest disagreements and unresolved moral dilemmas will remain. People of conscience may support different views of what moral duty entails, for equally good but conflicting reasons. Given this possibility, and given that people would still respect the need for conscience and for the deliberative mentality that is one essential ground for its authority, it is necessary that citizens be skeptical of moving to unreflective, extreme positions that deny the importance of considering opposing views. In doing so, citizens must act in ways suggested by Arthur Kuflik, who says, "a morally thoughtful person will not think himself automatically justified in disobeying any law or policy with which he finds himself in moral disagreement. He recognizes that in deciding what to do there may be more to consider than the law or policy itself, for instance, the degree to which the question of its moral propriety admits of reasonable disagreement, the moral seriousness and sincerity of those who hold opposing views, the extent to which the established framework genuinely fosters the settlement of differences through reason and argument rather than through threats and deceptions."[12]

The liberal citizen who acts from a sense of moral duty always manifests through his civility a tolerance for the fact that others may differ with him and that others may have legitimate grounds for doing so. Still, the person of conscience does not let his tolerance for difference excuse the state from carefully considering the views held by people of conscience. It would not be sufficient for the state to say that it respects conscience simply by excusing individuals from acting in accordance with policies they disagree with. To manifest an enlarged quality, the state must demonstrate to these individuals that it has carefully considered in its deliberations the positions of those who disagree with its policies. Indeed, the state must demonstrate that it has made a serious attempt to accommodate the views of people of conscience. And there is no reason to assume that the liberal state lacks an ability or the will to conduct itself in this enlarged manner, as Abbott seems to wish to contend.

In carefully considering the views of people of conscience, an authorizing ground of conscience is secured, the enlarged culture of a liberal society. And as long as the state sustains the latter, it may disagree with and deny a particular claim of conscience held by a person, but still correctly expect to receive from that person a strong obligation.

5

The Signs of an Enlarged
Citizen-State Culture

I. FORMAL AND SUBSTANTIVE LEGITIMACY

In this chapter and the next, I discuss how governments must act toward their citizens in order to create a relationship to them that is based upon a commitment to maintain an enlarged political culture. Citizens who demand that the state manifest an enlarged quality as a condition for citizens having an obligation in a strong sense to the state must be able to point to those forms of conduct or "signs" which demonstrate that the state is in fact maintaining an enlarged quality. The main sign in this regard is that the state be both *formally and substantively legitimate*. The bulk of this discussion will concentrate upon what is required in the latter instance. The view taken here is that formal legitimacy by itself is not sufficient to justify a strong obligation from citizens, but in addition, the state must make formal legitimacy instrumental to achieving substantive legitimacy. The latter is the essence of an enlarged citizen-state relationship. First, to set up this discussion, a brief statement needs to be made concerning what is meant by formal legitimacy.

Determining if the state is *formally* legitimate requires that one assess its commitment, as Flathman says, to the rule of law, constitutionalism, and "the idea of individual rights" or what I have called respect for basic rights and liberties.[1] Constitutionalism means that the state has various offices, like courts, a legislature and an executive, and these institutions are to conduct themselves in keeping with constitutionally prescribed procedures. These offices have the legal authority to either establish the laws and general policies or to enforce them for a variety of issue areas, while protecting the basic rights and liberties. Regarding the latter, the offices of government, in particular the courts and legislatures, must have the legal authority to define the rules that pertain to the provision of various liberties. For instance, in providing freedom of speech, it is necessary to determine the rule that draws the line between protected speech and libel; in protecting freedom of thought, it is necessary to provide a rule that demonstrates when expression is protected and when it is not as in cases involving child pornography; in protecting the rights of the accused it is necessary to distinguish due process of law from abusive uses of authority by the state against the accused. Moreover, once the rules pertaining to the nature of particular rights have been written, the state must enforce these rules in like cases toward all citizens who fall within the purview of the rule. A state is formally legitimate, or acts from a commitment to the rule of law, then, when its officials do not violate constitutional procedures during the course of carrying out its legal authority, and when it defines and enforces its public policy objectives and laws in a manner that ensures that the rules that define the nature of basic rights and liberties are applied to all citizens without exception.

A citizen who holds rights in a formal sense, or in the sense that he knows that the rules pertaining to the definition of rights are to be applied to him in the same way as to other citizens, may hope to use these rights to create sufficient independence from the government so that he can criticize government policy without fear of reprisal but with the assurance that his views are fully considered by policy officials. In particular, a citizen seeks to use the rights that are relevant to this objective, like the rights of speech, association, thought, conscience, and due process of law, to criticize and to evaluate the positions taken by policymakers in order to make changes in the public policy positions of the state. Here the citizen expects that policy officials understand that the formal guarantees associated with the rule of law will in fact ensure the basis for a *substantive* dimension to these rights, too.

Citizens may criticize existing policy or laws as manifesting tendencies which threaten to undermine basic conceptions of rights or they may argue against public policy positions on other grounds that do not involve questions or rights and liberties, such as that a certain law would destroy the physical environment in some critical way or that it would unduly inconvenience certain members of the community. Further, it is possible that citizens will question the rules that define rights and claim that these rules are either incomplete or unjust or that they set up a priority relationship between different rights that is unfair. In all cases, citizens who are engaged in this activity take the view that their rights give them the independence to make these critical evaluations and to expect that their views will be made a part of the policy process. If institutions do not foster a substantive use of rights, then citizens are denied the chance to be critically reflective persons, the state is seen as resisting a critically evaluative body politic, and citizens will rightfully judge the state as lacking in moral worth and say that the rights of persons have little or no significance.

In the rest of the chapter, I discuss various ways the state can manifest a commitment to rights in the substantive sense and thus act to maintain an enlarged citizen-state relationship as well. I do so by examining key political institutions, the role of the media, the voting process, and the challenge tradition. Finally, I conclude with a statement concerning the practical task of policy officials and citizens in preserving a very important form of an enlarged relationship to citizens, or what is called here public reason.

II. THE CITIZEN-STATE RELATIONSHIP

Before proceeding to discuss the signs of an enlarged citizen-state culture, a fact central to understanding the nature of the citizen-state relationship in a liberal state must be made clear. In doing so, I can then rule out certain kinds of signs as symbolic of a state's commitment to an enlarged culture. In particular, I can rule out as a basic sign the need for a form of participatory democracy.[2] In the next chapter, I will elaborate upon this point further, but for now the basis for this contention is that the state exists to most of its citizens as the governing authority, and it is as a governing authority that it makes policies that citizens may not directly participate in forming.

As the governing authority, the key way that a liberal state protects rights and liberties in both the formal and substantive sense is that it prevents a concentration of political power in the hands of any single actor or group of actors. In particular, the liberal state is divided into separate branches, each of which has a particular function in relation to the other branches. Here no one branch ends up with the lion's share of political power, but each branch must share its powers with the other branches.

Rights and liberties are protected formally, then, in a constitutionally balanced system where each branch carries out its functions in relation to procedures that prevent any branch from usurping all authority to itself. The legislature will make policies for the various issue areas, and, along with the courts, it will define rules for the provision of rights and liberties. The executive must make an application of the laws that is in keeping with legislative intent. In doing so, the executive must operate within the rules which have been established to secure basic rights and liberties by either the courts or the legislature. Finally, the courts monitor the actions of the other branches to ensure that neither the executive nor the legislative branch destroys the balance between each. In part, courts perform this function by ensuring that the rules that secure rights and liberties are uniformly applied. At other times, courts perform this task by defining the rules for providing rights and liberties, especially for those areas where they have responsibility for doing so, like in matters pertaining to criminal due process of law, speech, assembly, and so forth.

The most important part of the constitutional balance is that citizens have a chance to ensure that their views are carefully considered in the lawmaking and law administration process. When they are, then rights and liberties that provide this opportunity have been given substantive expression. The key elements in this process are a court system that protects basic citizen rights and a legislative branch that allows citizens to use these rights to secure a fair hearing for their views. When constitutional balance is undermined, it is likely that a substantive use of rights will be undermined, too. Indeed, it is the purpose of constitutional balance to remove the obstacles to full consideration by policymakers of citizen views.

A fuller explanation of this view will be provided in section 4 of the next chapter. For now the point is that entrenched interests may endanger an enlarged dimension to the policy-making process because they create a *corporatist* relationship between the state and its citizens. In this relationship, interest groups may gain the ability to determine policies pertaining to their own interests, excluding other parts of the public to the process, and they may even control administrative agencies that apply these policies to themselves. In this case, their members gain positions of importance at critical points in the legislative and administrative processes, and from these locations they can have influence on the public agenda denied to other citizens. As a consequence of this activity, the legislature's duty to define policies and the executive's duty to implement them are usurped and constitutional balance is placed in jeopardy.

Corporatist forms of political power allow specified interests to rig the policy structure in a way that permanently favors themselves and as a result denies a hearing to other views. This is especially the situation where the financial cost of political participation is so high that it excludes the average citizen. Political leaders and institutions must reduce the influence of this kind of entrenched power on the policy process because this situation not only may frustrate the effort to have formal rights, but it will certainly undermine an enlarged citizen-state relationship by denying rights in a substantive sense.

III. THE STATE AND MEDIA SIGNS OF ENLARGED THINKING

If citizens do not possess adequate information about the government, they may lack an understanding of possible corporatist tendencies within the government. Indeed, if the state begins to take on a corporatist form, then it is likely that the image it creates for itself is designed to hide this fact from the public. That is why the state must help maintain an independent public information system that acts as critic of the government and that works to expose its actual manner of operation. But even the actors of an independent media system may fail to provide a true picture of government activity. It may become co-opted by corporatist elements which would subvert the objective of providing the "truth" about the government to the citizens.

To prevent this possibility, the government must maintain what Giovanni Sartori calls the basis for an autonomous public opinion.[3] To do so, in addition to multiple sources of information, there must be a system of education that is "not a system of indoctrination."[4] In this setting public opinion "derives from, and is sustained by, a *polycentric structuring* of the media and by their *competitive interplay.*"[5] Implicit in this view is that the media present their material before a discriminating public whose chief concern is to understand what in fact is taking place within government. To this end, the public compares the different messages it receives from the various centers of information in an effort to determine which ones are most reliable and most useful in helping citizens find out the truth. This orientation creates a strong incentive for each agency of the media to make a sincere effort to find and report the truth, for unless it does, it may lose its audience to other media agencies doing a better job.

By helping to make this kind of information culture available to citizens the state manifests an important sign of an enlarged culture; in particular, it demonstrates that the basis for making decisions should be a culture in which all the diverse views can be carefully considered. Moreover, the state in promoting a competitive media atmosphere hopes that citizens will learn the importance of predicating judgments on an accurate factual basis. Indeed, in developing the quest to base judgments on accurate information, the culture as a whole gains an appreciation for those forms of public education that teach citizens the accepted methods and procedures for determining the accuracy of facts and for testing the propositions based upon them. This concern becomes the basis for a special political form of enlarged thinking, public reason, discussed in section 5. Finally, in this culture the government experiences constantly the kind of pressure on itself that would secure an enlarged approach to issues, and this enlarged approach helps it to protect rights in a substantive sense.

IV. THE CIVIL CHALLENGE TRADITION

In the view presented here, citizens live in relation to a state that governs them, and it is possible that they will never actually take direct part in the governing process. Yet if the state has an enlarged relationship to its citizens, it is able to openly and fully consider the broad array of citizen views on issues and thus protect citizen rights in a substantive way.

The most immediately important means that citizens have to ensure that their views are fully considered is the election process itself. Sartori argues that elections do not "enact policies; elections establish, rather, who will enact them."[6] However, while it is true that the electorate understands that one of its most critical tasks is to elect people who decide issues, it is also true that the electorate hopes through its vote to instruct the people whom it elects on what stances to take on the key issues that were discussed during the election. Indeed, elections are often framed in terms of the question, Do you want to keep the policies of the past or do you want to have them changed, and if the latter, in what direction do you want them changed? Those who are elected in this context by the efforts of a certain coalition of voters are likely to reflect the attitudes of those who elect them, and in deciding issues, it is quite likely to be the case that they will attempt to put into policy the views of the coalition that supported them.[7]

But it is also clearly the case that many issues elected officials face were not fully discussed before the election nor made a part of a winning candidate's agenda. Indeed, many issues emerge as important only after the election takes place. In these matters, the elected officials, after consulting widely with the coalition that elected them and with others, must decide for the electorate as a whole.

These realities place the electorate in a situation where it must manifest its approval or disapproval of the decisions that are arrived at by the elected officials. Moreover, if the attitude is one of disapproval and if there is no election in the offing, it becomes clear that elections are not always frequent enough to permit citizens a chance to manifest their opinions about the performance of elected officials. Public officials may be granted reprieves from citizen judgments for long periods, and this fact allows them to escape the scrutiny that many citizens may feel is necessary.

However, citizens have other means of registering evaluations (especially negative ones) of elected officials and these ways help to place their views before the elected officials for consideration. If one understands the citizen–elected official relationship as defined in terms of the citizen having a right to challenge the elected officials to publicly justify the latters' decisions, then the citizen can interact with and even affect the decision process through what I refer to as the challenge tradition. Elected officials must demonstrate respect for this tradition if, in fact, they are to maintain an enlarged relationship to the citizens.

Thus, if elections do not offer a fully adequate opportunity to challenge authority or if it appears that policymakers are in some sense intransigent in their willingness to consider citizen concerns, citizens can challenge state decisions in a civil manner. The tradition that best facilitates this possibility is the activity of civil protest embodied within the practice of civil disobedience. In the latter, citizens violate particular laws in order to protest grave injustices that they would like to see eradicated. Civil disobedience may be used to protest the state's failure to provide equal rights and liberties, as in the civil rights movement, or it may be used to protest other forms of "injustice." The latter may include matters like environmental concerns, income distribution questions, nuclear weapons matters, the practice of a state's use of covert intelligence, and so on.[8]

Civil challengers who engage in civil disobedience, as we indicated in the last chapter, indicate by their civil forms of protest that they do not want to threaten the state's authority. Further, civil challengers expect that when they conduct themselves civilly the state will create room for their activity and do its utmost to tolerate it. Practically, this means that civil challengers who practice civil disobedience by violating particular laws recognize that they must pay the penalty for such action, and in fact they are always willing to do so. But the penalties in these cases must not be harsh or severe. A state that places civil challengers in maximum security prisons for many years demonstrates that its intent is to block their interaction with the public. In this case, the state's concern is not to respond to the sincerity of civil challengers by recognizing that they have arguments that must be considered in the same spirit of civil conduct that they were provided. Rather, the intent is to end the challenge tradition, and when this intent becomes clear to citizens, the state loses moral worth because it no longer is able to create an enlarged relationship between itself and its citizens.

Further, it should also be clear that civil challengers need not always resort to civil disobedience to challenge the state's decisions. Civil challengers always hold this tactic as one option, but it is possible that their views will get a hearing even without resort to civil disobedience. The civil challengers may merely engage in legal public education campaigns to win support for their positions.

In either event, the purpose of the civil challenger's activity is to encourage the public to rethink its current views on a question. The process of civil challenge to authority begins, then, when a civil challenger appeals to the majority or to an active minority to reconsider a policy of the state and then to demand that the policymakers to do the same. The civil challenger succeeds initially when he is able to have a part of the public rethink its views and then, based on this new public understanding, to lobby for reconsideration by public officials. A gap between the public and the government would emerge if the state did not consider the civil challenger's claims. If the policymakers fail to seriously reconsider the challenged policy, then the challenge tradition is made useless, even if it has been guaranteed as a formal citizen right. But when the policymakers respond to the demands of the public inspired by the civil challenger, then the enlarged culture is preserved.

By "respond" in this case, what is meant is that the appropriate government body takes up the issue and fully considers it. In doing so, those views symbolized by the civil challenger are brought into the process of decision making. This process was exemplified in the 1930s by labor protests. The government could have taken the position that the union movement would not be considered at all in its determination of legislation dealing with business and labor relations. Instead, the state, in particular the Congress and the president, considered the labor view and passed legislation that became a bill of rights for labor and institutionalized the importance of the labor view in the political process.

Another example of what it means for government to respond took place in the civil rights period. When the civil rights movement first began, nearly all requests for redress were considered extreme and would be denied. Politicians said that civil rights activists who had the right to protest were moving "too fast," and that they should be content with more moderate solutions. But it became clear to the public that the issues raised by the civil rights activists were justified and that they were not receiving a full hearing. Until they were given this hearing, then the citizens could justifiably say that the state did not fully meet its commitment to provide a right (on both the formal and substantive levels) to challenge authority. In this case, in fact, the state was viewed as losing its right to elicit from its citizens a strong commitment to its laws. National political leaders averted this demise of respect for the state by bringing up the demands at the national level, in particular in the legislative and judicial processes, and this culminated in landmark laws that demonstrated the commitment to a fair consideration of civil challenger views.

V. CONCLUSION: THE ROLE OF PUBLIC REASON

From the preceding it is possible to make a clear statement about the practical tasks that governments and public officials must perform in an enlarged setting. The examples just provided from the civil challenge tradition demonstrate that the electorate and the public officials, in so far as they are able to maintain the traditions of an enlarged culture, constantly help to expand awareness of the types of concerns that must be included in the discussion of policy undertaken by public officials. This means public officials not only must consider fully different views that are already a part of the present discourse, but they must expand their range of concerns to include views that are not now granted full acceptance but that the civil challenger says should be made a part of that discourse.

For instance, before the civil rights movement, race policy was a matter for public discussion and decision. But the views surrounding this discussion only had to do with the best ways to maintain racial separation. The whole question of creating an integrated society based on the notion of full rights and liberties for all was nearly kept off the public agenda until the civil rights movement. Similarly with labor, prior to the labor activism of the 1930s, labor questions revolved around how best to maintain management autonomy and control. It was only the challenge brought forth from labor itself that expanded the debate to include the wider issues of the rights of labor.

For the state to have resisted efforts to include these concerns, as it did at one time, was for it to manifest its lack of a willingness to move beyond past notions of what was and was not an acceptable view to be considered in the public debate. The state was resisting an enlargement of the discussion. But in refusing to suppress enlargement of the discussion, the boundaries of discourse are expanded. Just how far these boundaries are expanded depends upon the ability of the civil challenger to convey and to convince and the willingness of the public to listen and to be convinced. In a setting where citizens have an enlarged mentality, as argued in chapter 3, there should be an easy receptivity to listen and to carefully consider all known positions on all issues that come before the public.

Further, whether the public can develop in this expanded discourse a common or a comprehensive agreement is of course another question. Perhaps as a result of the activities of the civil challenger, the public will develop a consensus. This seemed to be the case in the civil rights movement where a strong national consensus for civil rights legislation grew out of the protest activities. But it is just as possible that a civil challenger's actions may help to cause the emergence, from those who disagree with the civil challenger, of opposing views. This outcome was often found during the Vietnam period. It is true that the public became disaffected with the war, inspired in part by the civil challenge to it. But there were wide differences of opinion concerning how to get out of the war, with some hoping for a Viet Cong victory, others hoping for a peace that secured a U.S.-backed government in the South, and still others demanding total victory over the North by a stepped up war effort that would place the South in control of all of Vietnam.

The practical task of government, in matters where differences of view exist on an issue, is to seek to resolve the differences and to find agreement while maintaining an enlarged relationship to its citizens. In pursuing a consensus, public officials hope to find a general agreement on the basic principles that should govern the approach taken to an issue. In a liberal society for matters pertaining to issues that touch on rights and liberties, the nature of the consensual principle is clear: it is necessary to provide rights and liberties to all. But not all issues will have to do with rights and liberties. Matters pertaining to disputes about the proper approach to conservation of environmental resources, air pollution, or national defense, for instance, may only touch on how best to define a notion of the public good, and citizens will search for the consensual principles which can be the foundation of an agreement.

When public officials or citizens use enlarged thinking to resolve political issues, enlarged thinking can be called "public reason."[9] Public officials seek the consensual principles that should govern decisions in matters not dealing with rights and liberties, and for those that do, they seek to realize the principle of providing rights and liberties for all. In either case, once the principles are determined, public reason seeks a policy which can best embody the principles in question.

These inquiries are governed by some important traditions. The most important is that in framing the discussion public officials hope to avoid arguments that seek to win support merely by triggering favorable emotions and passions in others. Instead, public officials hope to put forth rational arguments that convince others of the weakness of certain views and of the strength of others. To accomplish this purpose public officials use accepted techniques for gathering evidence, and they make use of accepted procedures for verifying propositions based on the evidence. In thinking in this way, a competitive dialogic context emerges in which the various parties hope to "woo" each other to their side. In the process, public officials, as they look at the issue from the point of view of opponents, may modify their views and possibly even adopt the view of their opponents. It should be clear, however, that the basis for this change of mind is that the opponent's arguments appear to provide convincing reasons, reasons that from the standpoint of the person being convinced should persuade others too.

Several additional factors about the tradition of public reason emerge at this point. First, citizens and public officials who engage in public reason have a disposition to try to search for the "truth" in the arguments of opponents. This means that they will strive to understand the views that differ from their own. Further, this attitude also means that one adopts a compromising aura in public reason without being compromised. By this I mean that liberal citizens and public officials understand that at times to reach an agreement on either a consensual principle or on an application of one they will have to meet others halfway and modify their views somewhat by encompassing aspects of the other person's arguments, even if they do not fully agree with them.

Thus in the matter pertaining to what to do, if anything, to help the working poor, there is a major consensual principle that liberal citizens and public officials would find acceptable; namely that all citizens should be treated fairly by being accorded full access to basic rights and liberties. The problem here is that citizens who work hard but who still find themselves at the poverty level may find themselves without a full opportunity to take advantage of these liberties. As a result of their inferior economic condition, they may not be able to make use of the right of political participation. They do not have the time to participate because of their work, nor do they have the finances necessary for effective participation.

Now the question is, What policy should be invoked to secure fairness for individuals who work hard but whose income is at or below the poverty level? Some may argue for a minimum income for the working poor. At first, I, as a public official, may not agree with other public officials arguing for a minimum income for all who fall below a certain level of income because I do not think the state acts fairly if it gives certain people special preference with respect to receiving income. How is this program fair to the lower middle class, for instance, whose members also do not have large amounts of wealth even though they work? If the concern is to provide equal political participation, then instead of a minimum income, why not make reforms of the political process to provide the working poor with full rights of participation? However, the proponents of a minimum convincingly argue that if we do not provide a minimum income to the working poor, then we have accepted a policy or application of the fairness principle that inordinately penalizes the children of the working poor. The proponents then document the experience of other countries who have instituted a minimum income.

After hearing the case made by proponents, in particular evidence that the children will have better opportunities for success if this plan is put into place, I decide to support this program on a trial basis. Once the trial is over the program will be reevaluated to see if it has worked. In this example, I have agreed to meet these proponents halfway. My acceptance of views that I previously rejected is based upon what appears to be well-established argumentation by those trying to convince me. I presume as proof of the argument's validity that others who similarly agreed with me in rejecting the contentions of those arguing for a minimum income, would also upon reflection be impressed with the soundness of the argument and agree to meet the argument halfway, too.

But even here there is likely to be a continuing dispute over whether this is the best way to achieve a general commitment to fairness. The accepted policy to provide a minimum income to the working poor, is still a subject of dispute as a result of the compromise. Perhaps fairness is best achieved when a minimum income is not supplied, and by requiring that the program will be reevaluated after a certain time, citizens hold open the possibility that upon close examination of the results of the program, it may be necessary to rescind it. Within a general commitment to fairness we have established a policy that some people strongly support and others are wary of. As a consequence of the debate, then, we have reached a very weak consensus, one that may be reversed later and certainly one that is subject to constant questioning and critique with an eye to revision.

This result is not untypical of debates in a liberal society. The process of public reason may produce agreement on policies for implementing consensual principles, but the consensus may be with so many reservations that the policy may have only weak support. Still, where the tradition of public reason is well established, citizens and public officials understand the limits of public reason and understand its importance nonetheless. In the first place, they recognize that there is nothing else to fall back on for making decisions. The overall commitment to fairness does not dictate how policies relating to the working poor should be decided, nor is there a system of principles displaying a Platonic unity that can make the decision for us. Further, if public officials decided based upon self-interest considerations alone, then they would not consider views that differed from their own, and in this case, they would undermine the prospect of providing rights in a substantive sense. As a consequence, the state could not develop toward its citizens an enlarged relationship; indeed, the state would close itself off from the views of those it represented by refusing to consider them.

An additional reason for fostering public reason, despite the possibility that it may only forge a weak consensus on many issues, is the knowledge that in attempting to grapple with diverse views, public officials labor to understand opposing views. This experience, the chief experience of public reason, reduces the psychological distance that might exist in public officials' minds with respect to opposing views, and in doing so public reason creates respect for diversity. Further, in constantly trying to accommodate diverse views, public officials demonstrate a long-term commitment to try to work out differences, and this consequence is in line with a central belief of citizens that society should be a cooperative setting. Indeed, in practicing public reason, public officials live up to the expectation of liberal citizens that society should be a cooperative arrangement that is organized to permit different citizens to contribute to other members in vital ways, and that, further, society should be concerned to work out disagreements over how best to achieve this end.

6

A Critique of
Participatory Theories

I. THE MAIN ARGUMENT

For Sartori, the concept of a participatory, democratic politics holds, among other things, that citizens should have "real and effective participation in decision making."[1] To achieve this impact, citizens must have, to use Rawls's terms, equal political liberty and equal worth of political liberty. For Rawls, equal political liberty, which Rawls also refers to as the principle of equal participation,[2] means the provision of liberties such as the freedoms of speech and assembly, the liberties of thought and conscience, the right to influence the agenda, and the right to a public forum that is open to all.[3] The problem in providing these rights is that often "the liberties protected by the principle of political participation lose much of their value [or worth] whenever those who have greater private means are permitted to use their advantages to control the course of public debate."[4] Over time, these people would gain "larger influence over the development of legislation."[5] To prevent this from happening, institutions and policies that secure the "fair value" (or worth) of equal political liberty for all are necessary. By securing a fair value to political liberty, Rawls means that the liberal society must "secure a fair opportunity to take part in and to influence the political process [and] those similarly endowed and motivated should have roughly the same chance of attaining positions of political authority irrespective of their economic and social class."[6] To achieve a fair value to liberty in this sense, Rawls suggests permitting government funds for public discussion; distributing ownership of private property, wealth, and means of production across society; and maintaining political party independence from private economic interests.[7]

Rawls's proposals are designed to avoid unequal worth of political liberty among ordinary citizens, but one might ask, Should we worry about the unequal worth of liberty between citizens and officeholders? Clearly, once in office, an officeholder's political liberty, owing to his legal authority, will have greater worth than a nonofficeholder's. This outcome concerns Rawls less than the loss of the equal value of political liberty among ordinary citizens. Rather, when he turns his attention to legislators, for instance, his main concern is that the representatives must "seek first to pass just and effective legislation," and "they must further their constituents' other interests insofar as these are consistent with justice."[8] Rawls does not discuss the implications for the principle of equal political participation of officeholders having superior power to make policy. Part of the reason for his not doing so perhaps is his belief that "in a well-governed state only a small fraction of persons may devote much of their time to politics. There are many forms of human good. But this fraction, whatever its size, will most likely be drawn more or less equally from all sectors of the society. The many communities of interests and centers of political life will have their active members who look after their concerns."[9]

But critiques of liberalism from the standpoint of participatory theory would see the unequal worth of liberty between officeholders and citizens as a problem, too. If all people have equal liberty to run for office, and if after the election the winners have greater liberty to make policy than the losers, then our political liberties have been made unequal in worth. Participatory theorists critique liberal regimes precisely on these grounds. Their arguments suggest that citizens should make decisions on many of the major issues that elected officials decide. For instance, why not have citizens decide through a referendum if there should be a tax increase, a defense buildup, or a new welfare plan? In this case, citizens would have equal worth of liberty to those whom they elect as public officials. Participatory theories then make a case for restoring the worth of the liberty of participation by providing political reforms such as permitting referenda on public issues (which I take to be the key mechanism of participatory democracy, as I argue in section 5), more intensive civic education, limiting the impact of money on politics, and more union democracy, factory democracy, and local neighborhood democracy, and so forth.[10]

All of these devices are laudable, and from the standpoint of liberal theory, some might be useful for restoring equal worth of political liberty among citizens. But even with them, the fact remains that in matters pertaining to policy-making, certain persons in a liberal state, in particular duly certified public officials, will have greater worth to their political liberty than will average citizens. If that is the case, does this mean that the liberal state loses its right to claim citizens' respect and a strong citizens' sense of obligation, based on the argument that rights and liberties lose their value in a liberal state if political liberties among citizens and policymakers are not of equal worth?

My answer is no, and I use an argument usually given on behalf of participatory theory to defend the liberal regime against participatory critiques. Participatory theories imply that when citizens do not have a similar worth of liberty as policymakers, they cannot engage in the discourse of policy-making and as a result gain for themselves an ability to think in enlarged terms as well as form policy that reflects an enlarged understanding. My contention is that even if citizens do not have the same actual worth of political liberty as policymakers, they can still understand political liberty as having fair worth if the basic rights and liberties in a liberal state are arranged to permit citizens, either through the challenge tradition or through the actions of public officials, to remove the corporatist impediments to basing policy on the discourse of public reason. If this is the case, then citizens possess precisely what participatory theorists would hope for as a result of direct citizen participation in politics: an ability to base society's politics on an enlarged understanding. I trace out these lines of argument in the sections that follow.

II. BARBER AND PATEMAN

Benjamin Barber and Carole Pateman argue that the institutions that facilitate a general obligation to political authority are ones which permit a participatory form of politics. For Pateman, an obligation as ordinarily understood is always a "self-assumed" requirement, and participatory settings maintain this understanding of the term for political settings by permitting people to assume or to freely choose their own obligations.[11] Here, participation is a form of political practice that creates a "relationship of political obligation that is owed by each citizen to his or her fellow citizens."[12]

Barber, in a similar vein, says that a strong democracy emphasizes "common participatory activity," and "common talk" that makes possible a "creative consensus" formed from the "cooperative" and

"active" endeavors of the members.[13] Moreover, as a result of participating in forming policies, citizens develop very strong attachments to
what they have helped to create, and further, these strong attachments
signify that citizens have strong obligations to uphold the policies they
help to construct. Indeed, the strength of citizens' obligation is indicated by the fact that their identities as particular persons are
informed by the need to incorporate, as an essential aspect of their
character as persons, the norms and the notion of the commonly held
purposes of the community. Thus Barber says, a "strong democracy
creates the very citizens it depends upon *because* it depends upon
them, because it permits the representation neither of *me* nor of *we*
because it mandates a permanent confrontation between the *me* as
citizen and the "Other" as citizen, forcing *us* to think in common
and act in common. The citizen is by definition a *we* thinker, and to
think of the *we* is always to transform how interests are perceived and
goods defined."[14]

Seen against this background, liberal society has severe shortcomings. The main problem is that even as liberal political philosophy
sanctions a voluntarist basis for obligation, liberal political institutions
fail to live up to this standard because they do not provide equal worth
of political liberty between citizens and public officials. And this fact
is demonstrated throughout the major political institutions that permit citizen input into the policy-making process. Thus, for Barber
representative government is "incompatible with freedom because it
delegates and thus alienates political will at the cost of genuine self-
government and autonomy."[15] Similarly for Pateman,"the job of the
elected representative is precisely to take political decisions for, to
impose political obligations upon, the community as a whole. Thus
political obligation is an exception to the general conception of obligation as self-assumed obligation; the individual actor decides when to
make a promise (oblige himself), the (few) representatives decide
when political obligations will be incurred. That political obligation is,
in general problematical in the liberal democratic state, is because the
question can always be asked from within the assumptions of liberal
theory itself, why the individual actor's political obligation should
differ from his other obligations."[16]

In each case, citizens find themselves losing to others the power
to make binding decisions on their own lives. Consequently, for both
writers liberal political institutions or representative government are
tied to an unequal worth of basic political liberties. In particular, the
liberty of representatives and political officials has greater worth than
that of the citizens who must live with the impact of their decisions.

Still, this is but one sign of the unequal worth of political liberty. Writers like Barber see others. For instance, the important institution of voting cannot provide citizens equal worth of political liberty with those who govern them. Barber says that voting has become a narrow private act in which people are encouraged to register only a definition of their own statement of private interest maximization. Voting is like "using a public toilet: we wait in line with a crowd in order to close ourselves up in a small compartment where we can relieve ourselves in solitude and in privacy of our burden, pull a lever, and then, yielding to the next in line, go silently home,"[17] Seen in this way, our governors can use the voting process to manipulate citizens in ways that benefit mostly themselves and thus perpetuate their greater worth of liberty.

For Pateman, to eliminate unequal worth of liberty there must be direct or participatory voting. "In participatory or self-managing democracy, citizens, collectively, exercise political authority over themselves in their capacity as private individuals; or, to make this point in a different way, in voting they are subordinating themselves to their own collective judgment, not the judgment of others."[18] Pateman seems to make a plea here for referendum democracy, which would allow citizens to take direct part in shaping major policy decisions on important issues. Here, instead of voting for others who vote on these issues, citizens would vote directly on the issues themselves, and by doing so overcome the impediments imposed by a liberal state's unequal worth of political liberty between citizens and elected officers.

Participatory practices can be understood as ways to avoid this problem. By providing chances for citizens to participate directly in the policy-making process, unequal worth of political liberty can be eliminated. Moreover, for these practices to be genuine, citizens must use them not so much to make politics promote only personal preferences, but to work with others to create a common political future. Citizens would display in the judgments they developed the capacity for what I have called enlarged thinking.

This outcome seems to be Barber's intent when he says that liberal societies are "thin" democracies, in which "citizens are spectators and clients while politicians are professionals who do the actual governing—in other words, [thin democracy offers] an understanding of democracy not as collective self-government but as the rule of elites who are periodically legitimized by elections."[19] In this view, as clients and spectators citizens are encouraged to see public life as a vehicle through which to realize private needs as opposed to defining and pursuing public goods and needs.[20] But in a strong democracy there is a form of political talk, to use Barber's term for what I have called public reason, and political talk creates the conditions for commonality. In particular, political talk is nourished by empathy, and empathy has a "politically miraculous power to enlarge perceptions and expand consciousness in a fashion that not so much accommodates as transcends private interests and the antagonisms they breed."[21]

Political talk in Barber's strong democracy, because it embodies empathy, teaches people who engage in it to become "kin" by virtue of their "common language" rather than adversaries as a consequence of their "divergent interests."[22] People may bargain or as Barber says "exchange benefits," but because the bargaining is complemented by a more "complex, open-ended art of conversation,"[23] there is an attempt to approach differences through a form of mutual exploration.[24] In this case, the concern is not just finding what is mutually beneficial, but defining the "common context, traits, circumstances, or passions that make of two separate identities one single *we*."[25] Political talk would not place in jeopardy the quest of public reason, defined in the last chapter, for a cooperative setting that could make possible a respect for diversity. Indeed, political talk could help to create and sustain this setting by reducing the psychological distance among people and by helping people to see each other as potential contributors to a cooperative setting that makes respect for protecting diverse forms of life possible.

Here, as in the case of public reason, citizens rely on political talk to decide issues because judgments must be made on a variety of matters, in the absence as Barber says of an independent ground "from which the concepts, values, standards, and ends of political life can be derived by simple deduction."[26] Even if an independent ground for political judgments (or what I called in chapter 2 a Platonic structure of integrated concepts) cannot be found, political judgments can still be made by citizens who formulate their own views only after giving a full hearing to other views. The nature of political talk, as demonstrated in previous chapters, emphasizes the search for what is common and shared among the diverse views encountered. Political talk symbolizes an ability and intention of people to put themselves in the place of others and to work to determine a common purpose or good.[27]

Political talk is to help people to minimize the distortions of self-interest and prejudice during the course of opinion formation. Citizens, in testing their views against those held by others, are able to make their own views less a manifestation of their own prejudices and more a statement of commonly accepted ideas. As a consequence of this experience, citizens come to transform themselves from self-interested "me" thinkers into "we" thinkers, supportive of community norms that all help create. Citizens predicate their judgments on the assumption that their own views are limited and that to make them more whole they must participate with others in a discussion that allows people to compare and contrast their own views with those held by others. This form of talk helps people to discover common bonds and to create a basis for a life that permits people to ensure that their private self works in harmony with the public norms of the society.

Barber's political talk is inventive, and thus it becomes the basis for creating "alternative futures,"[28] especially in settings where prior to the talk the divergent interests appeared only to lead to a status quo that few accepted but that few had any hope of overcoming. Still, it is possible that after the talk takes place, some will disagree with the consensus that emerges. If people do, however, they will not see the community as alien to their interests. As a consequence of political talk, they will feel bound by the results, even as they feel free to challenge them and to thus "keep the issue on the public agenda,"[29] as well as the search for the common good. As in the process of public reason, political talk, as a form of enlarged thinking, enables people to support common purposes even when they disagree with them. In this case, political talk signifies that citizens can in a strong democracy (as well as in a liberal society) work to change the consensus they disagree with, even as they agree to abide by it. Political talk, like public reason, then, makes possible a continuing commonality among citizens of diverse views, each of whom is working to help create a common good all can support.[30]

Pateman also emphasizes the importance of public reason in her view of participatory democracy, and like Barber she implies the need for equal political liberty and equal worth of liberty among policymakers and citizens. But her view of participatory democracy emphasizes the centrality of the notion of promise in everyday life to the notion of political obligation. Thus, to understand her concept of political obligation, it is necessary to recognize that underlying Pateman's discussion is the assumption that "political obligation is a form of promising, or if it can be validly compared to a promise, then there is no doubt that it is indeed 'obligation,' like the obligations that individuals assume in their everyday lives."[31] The concept of making promises in private matters can be used to understand Pateman's concept of political obligation as long as the differences between the two

notions are carefully distinguished. Making promises in private matters is understood as an act in which two or more people, from their
own free will, mutually agree to uphold certain forms of conduct with
respect to each other. In politics citizens should have the same
freedom to form their own notion as to what kinds of laws and
policies they wish to live under. The difference between promises in
private matters and those in public ones is that in public ones citizens
order their own lives by voting [or what appears to be referendum
democracy], which "enables citizens to decide on the basis of their
own deliberations and judgment to create a relationship of obligation
in their political lives."[32]

What is similar in each form of promising is that people should
be able to enter into it and assume an obligation on the basis of their
own freely formed judgments.[33] Further, to make a promise presumes
that the course we choose is the best we can determine after a period
of reflection and judgment. Thus insofar as promising means our
agreeing to take on an obligation, it means first and foremost our
desire to make a judgment in a clear state of mind about what course
of conduct is best for us. Pateman draws from the ordinary view of
promising the same kind of lesson for political promising, as
manifested in participatory settings. The latter assumes that citizens
"are capable of independent judgments and rational deliberation, and
of evaluating and changing their own views of actions and relationships."[34] We wish, in other words, to live a life guided by the best
judgments we are capable of making.

If this implication of Pateman's argument is to be taken seriously,
there is a lesson to be gained from the participatory experience. Thus,
using the analogy to personal promising, a major reason why we, as
citizens, would demand the right to help determine the nature of the
laws that govern us, or the reason why we would do best to think as
members of a community determining the basis for a shared way of
life, is that we wish to be sure that the final judgments that govern us
are made in the light of the most informed and fullest possible
understanding of a situation.

Once again, as in Barber, the basis for good judgments about
political or public matters is the public discourse that allows persons
to engage each other in a form of thinking that allows the limitations
of their own views to be transcended. In the process, citizens see
themselves not solely as holders of individual interests, but as community members who need one another for developing clear, non-
distorted judgments about their public life. Only as a result of non-

distorted, enlarged discourse can citizens have a clear understanding of the issues that confront them, and only then can they make confident judgments.

III. PARTICIPATION AND ENLARGED THOUGHT

From this discussion, the central importance to participatory theory of an enlarged culture is made clear. Political judgments in these settings are aided by the fact that they are not distorted either by false conceptions of an independent standard or by distorted visions of individuals who refuse to test their views against others'. These factors enlarge the discussion in a manner favorable to creating a more comprehensive statement of the common good.

Further, because political judgments can only be made when each of the various interests in a community are carefully considered, persons develop an expectation that their views and those of others too will be respected and that every effort will be made to accommodate them. When this expectation is met, people can feel that they are a politically important part of the society, precisely because their views are respectfully addressed by the other members and by public officials. Citizens are likely to feel that because their views are carefully considered, the regime under which they live is one that can be effective in making their views an integral part of the policy process.

IV. LIBERAL POLITICS AND THE ENLARGED CITIZEN-STATE RELATIONSHIP

The challenge posed to liberalism from participatory theories is if the liberal regime, which protects basic rights and liberties and which does so without necessitating equal worth of political liberties between citizens and policymakers, can facilitate a state that has an enlarged relationship to its citizens.

The gist of an enlarged relationship between citizens and public officials is that the former are able to get the latter to seriously consider and then to act upon the views which emerge from the public reason of citizens and public officials. In this case, public reason manifests itself as a politically effective form of conduct in which the opinions that emerge from within society's enlarged discourse have actual impact in shaping policy. The enlarged culture makes as its priority a citizen-state relationship whose essential feature is that as a result of an enlarged approach to issues, citizens actually become empowered, and with this power they actually affect public policy in a manner that reflects the conclusions of public reason.

This is an important characteristic of an enlarged citizen-state rapport because it is an unfortunate reality of liberal states that there are often impediments in the policy-making process that prevent the voice of public reason from having any impact on policy. The liberal state, as a consequence of its decisions to make government a provider of essential services like defense, social welfare, agricultural benefits, and so on, has developed a large administrative machinery to manage programs authorized by the legislature.

The problem is that certain administrative agencies, which are bolstered by powerful interest groups, often develop a political agenda and strategy to overturn constitutional balance as they promote a corporatist relationship to the state and gain their own political independence from the legislative process. In this situation, instead of the legislature determining public policy objectives, an administrative agency seeks to do so without interference from the legislature. Legislative bodies are especially susceptible to these violations of legislative authority because there are many places within legislative bodies that offer administrative agencies a chance to prevent the formation of a broad and powerful consensus to support legislation that returns the authority to make policy back to the legislative body. For instance, in the United States Congress the complexity of the committee system disperses decision authority to a great many actors. Each committee or subcommittee can provide a chance for a powerful minority to veto actions which would lead to the development of a powerful consensus to restore constitutional balance and to overcome a corporatist dimension to politics.

A state has an enlarged citizen-state relationship when it can overcome these impediments to constitutional balance. In this culture, perhaps through the actions of the civil challenger, or perhaps as a consequence of political leadership in the executive or legislative branches of government, a discourse based on public reason is established between the state officials and the citizenry. Each is given a chance to hear diverse views concerning how best to achieve fairness in a particular policy arena, say taxation. After a careful comparing of views in the manner required by public reason, let's say that there is a general, public agreement that tax policies should be changed in a direction that threatens the activities of certain administrative agencies like defense or agriculture. However, to do so requires that the administrative agencies with strong veto power located at various points in the legislative process be overruled. To accomplish this, political leaders, affected by the consensus that has arisen from the process of public reason, then define their mission as working to achieve within the legislative setting a powerful consensus that can disarm the veto power of these agencies and their constituencies. If the effort is successful, the enlarged citizen-state relationship, which starts with the process of public reason, has moved to a more advanced level now that the actions of public officials to overturn administrative agency intransigence and to restore constitutional balance have been successful. This action actually empowers citizens and demonstrates in the process that the enlarged culture has once again been vindicated, and as a result, citizens have every reason to continue to remain obligated in a strong sense to its authority.

V.   REFERENDUM DEMOCRACY AND UNEQUAL WORTH OF LIBERTY

Certainly, if it were possible, it would be highly desirable to have the society govern itself on the basis of equal political liberty with equal worth of that liberty. The closest that any liberal society can come to that objective is when there is an enlarged citizen-state relationship. But even in this case, it is true that citizens do not have and will not have the same power to shape policy as do the public officials. The enlarged citizen-state relationship provides citizens with fair worth of liberty only. But it must be said that participatory settings, even if they could be established in society, could do no better. This contention is best understood when articulated in terms of the main institutional practice that participatory theorists might claim as the basis for permitting equal worth of liberty, referendum democracy.

Indeed, direct participation in government decision making suggests a form of referendum democracy. Pateman would have to subscribe to this form of citizen participation, given her commitment to "participatory or self-managing democracy," as we have already indicated. Barber hopes to expand the initiative and referendum process to encompass more issues, and he makes this a central reform of the liberal state.[35] The usual criticism of this form of participation is that citizens lack the competence to vote on all the major issues before society. Further, it is claimed that participation will not necessarily increase voter competence, but it will in fact encourage greater degrees of passion and emotion, thus causing less, not more, rational decision making.[36]

Participatory theorists argue against these criticisms, saying that the public does have the competence to make important decisions, and further, that in taking part in them citizens enhance their knowledge and competence.[37] Participatory theorists have a point here. Political issues, however complex, can be explained, and choices and their consequences can be articulated in a manner that allows the average citizen to make an enlarged judgment about them. But in saying this, what becomes clear as well is that those who do the explaining or those who help initiate the challenge are key actors in the process. Without their leadership, there would be no public education or civic action.

The discussion of the role of either the civil challenger or the public official in an enlarged citizen-state relationship made precisely this point. The enlarged citizen-state relationship depends in large part upon the ability of the political leaders to successfully engage the public in a manner that inspires public reason. In this case, the success of an enlarged citizen-state culture depends not just on citizens having equal political liberty or fair worth of liberty (through the civil challenge process), but on the superior virtues, talents, and skills of political leadership. It is also true that for an enlarged citizen-state relationship to succeed, public officials who seek to incorporate the public consensus into policy must have superior worth of political liberty (in relation to average citizens) in order to remove the hindrances, such as those found in corporatist political practices, to achieving this objective. Similarly, to make the referendum process succeed in engendering citizen public reason requires the same leadership that is required for a successful enlarged citizen-state relationship; indeed the referendum process could well be a means by which to mount a civil challenge that helped to create an enlarged citizen-state relationship, and if it were, civic leadership would be pivotal to its success.[38] Citizens who have these abilities and who have a commitment to use them for promoting broad public involvement on issues would be the key to the success of referendum democracy. These citizens would act as civic leaders to direct public attention toward reducing the "disproportionate" influence of those groups whose power must be reduced if the publicly defined objectives are to be achieved. Civic leaders, to play this role, engender for themselves a greater worth to their equal political liberty in comparison to the average citizen.

In reality, participatory theorists would have to agree that the real issue between themselves and liberalism is not that one secures equal worth of political liberty and the other does not, but how to secure an enlarged culture in a setting where equal worth of liberty is not possible. Liberal regimes can sustain an enlarged relationship to citizens so long as the challenge tradition is kept strong and so long as there remains a strong tradition to resist corporatist tendencies within society and government. In this event, critiques of liberal theory from the participatory point of view have much less significance; and the real issue becomes the problem Rawls identifies, which is how to secure fair worth of political liberty in order to preserve (from the standpoint of the argument presented here) an enlarged culture.

7

The Social Learning Process
in a Liberal Regime

I. INTRODUCTION

This book has been written from the point of view of my particular construction of a "good" (and hopefully not mythical) liberal citizen. I have suggested since the first chapter that citizens in a liberal state would find the state's qualities desirable, and as a result they would wish to discover a basis to secure a strong obligation to its authority. But it is possible that the question of why one should be obligated to a liberal state may not be important to many ordinary citizens. These persons may look upon the rights and liberties liberal states provide with indifference. Were this attitude widespread, liberal citizens would discover a difficulty of equal magnitude to the problem discussed in chapter 1 of a liberal state that reacts to citizen refusals to maintain a strong obligation by becoming overly coercive, and in the process, undermining the character of the liberal regime. A state's liberal character also would be endangered if its citizens were by and large apathetic about requiring the state to maintain basic rights and liberties for all. To avert this apathy, the ideal liberal citizen desires a social learning process that can teach people to place a high value on these qualities of a liberal state and to expect the state to provide them. Furthermore, the social learning process that has this objective cannot achieve it by making people into passive servants of the state, a danger of any social learning process. This result would undermine the challenge tradition that is so vital to a liberal society. Thus, the task for a social learning process is to teach the importance of rights and liberties while nurturing the critically evaluative mind that is necessary to sustain the challenge tradition.

101

II. THE GENERAL ARGUMENT

So what is the best way to approach (and note I say "approach," since it is not my intent to describe the institutional setting that would achieve the objectives discussed here) a conception of a social learning process that teaches citizens to value a liberal society? My argument is that a social learning process based on Rawls's notion of moral psychology teaches the importance of liberal values by demonstrating that the development of persons takes place only in a setting that provides basic rights and liberties to all on a fair basis, the essence of Rawls's principles of justice.[1]

This general approach to social learning I develop from Rawls is built upon several important assumptions that Rawls makes in his description of an ideal concept of society, and that I, using Rawls's assumptions to support the need for a social learning process, make as well. Rawls's first important assumption is that Rawls's citizens live in a "well-ordered society." A "well-ordered" society is one in "which everyone accepts and knows that the others accept the same principles of justice, and the basic social institutions satisfy and are known to satisfy these principles."[2] This type of society is governed by principles that have a history of being an integral part of a liberal culture.[3] Second, one must also presume that a prime concern of persons is the desire to attain self-worth or self-respect. Rawls's principles of justice (described in footnote 1) distribute what he refers to as primary goods, which are rights and liberties, powers and opportunities, income and wealth, and self-respect. The latter primary good has "central place,"[4] and thus the other primary goods should be construed as important at least in part because they contribute to a society which makes self-respect possible. Here, liberal society is construed as I have described it too, as a setting in which basic rights and liberties contribute to the development of all persons. I assume, however, as the opening lines of this chapter indicate, a nonideal reality that permeates even Rawls's ideal concept of society; namely, that many citizens may become indifferent to Rawls's ideal assumptions. Therefore, I also assume a need for a social learning process that combats this indifference and its harmful effects by demonstrating the importance of a liberal society to its citizens. It does this by teaching people to value self-respect and what chiefly contributes to it, a society that secures rights and liberties for all.

Regarding this last assumption, linking the sense of self-worth to the provision of rights and liberties evolves in accordance with the concept of moral development that Rawls describes and that the social learning process would have to promote. And central to this social learning process is an enlarged culture. Rawls envisions a three-step phase in the moral development process. The three stages are the morality of authority, the morality of association, and the morality of principles. Each stage is associated with a sentiment that is peculiar to that stage and that supports the moral outlook associated with it. The morality of authority is linked to parent-child love, the morality of association to friendship and group solidarity, and the morality of principles to a sense of justice or fairness. The last stage is the most developed of the three, for in the last stage the basis for moral commitment is neither personal rapport among family members, nor friendship or solidarity among nonfamily members, but acceptance of and support for the principle of providing equal rights and liberties on a basis that contributes to self-respect for all. Taken together, these sentiments may be understood as a further elaboration of Smith's sentiment of sympathy (discussed in chapter 2), which like Rawls's sense of justice, will act as the basis for a discourse based on the aim of realizing fairness, discussed in section 4 of this chapter.

Each stage implies a different character to the moral outlook of citizens, and it is my contention that to attain the highest stage it is necessary that citizens be able to look upon society from an enlarged point of view that demonstrates the actuality of a cooperative setting founded on a commitment to basic rights and liberties and contributing to the self-worth of all persons. Without an enlarged standpoint, then citizens would become "stuck" at the level of the morality of either authority or association, they would not understand society as a cooperative arrangement based on rights and liberties that help to secure self-worth for all citizens, and as a consequence, persons would not be able to develop a commitment to support basic rights and liberties from a morality of principle.

At the center of this view of social learning is Rawls's "social union of social unions," or a "community of humankind the members of which enjoy one another's excellences and individuality elicited by free institutions, and they recognize the good of each as an element in the complete activity the whole scheme of which is consented to and gives pleasure to all."[5] I hope my interpretation of Rawls's view of moral development provides greater depth to this vision by demonstrating the central place of an enlarged culture to a social learning process that embodies Rawls's notion of moral development. I further hope that this vision will be more fully developed as a result of learning that the enlarged culture focus so central to Rawls's notion of moral development culminates in the discourse of fairness and makes this the central perspective of those committed to the "social union of social unions" ideal. Although in Rawls's account of moral development the importance of this perspective is not explicitly developed, it is nonetheless the case that the critical place of an enlarged viewpoint, especially as it is manifested in the discourse of fairness, cannot be denied. In the discussion that follows, I provide a reading of Rawls's moral psychology along these lines.[6]

III. THE STAGES OF THE MORAL CULTURE

In the morality of authority stage, parental love signifies that others exist to be "concerned for his [a child's] wants and needs" and to "affirm his sense of worth as his own person."[7] Moreover, parental love is "unconditional: they [parents] care for his [the child's] presence and spontaneous acts, and the pleasure they take in him is not dependent upon disciplined performances that contribute to the well-being of others." As a result of parental care, a child gains confidence in his surroundings and gains the wherewithal to "launch out and to test his maturing abilities."[8]

Knowing that parents really have concern for its self-worth, the child accepts the authority of its parents from a sense of love and trust.[9] Of course, the child, under the morality of authority, does not comprehend the "larger scheme of right and justice within which the rules addressed to him are justified."[10] The morality of authority is a primitive kind of morality, and it is based on virtues like "obedience, humility and fidelity to authoritative persons."[11]

Still, for Rawls the morality of authority can prepare children for the higher morality if it can avoid becoming a parochial influence that denies the possibilities of the nonfamily world for the development of persons. Indeed, the self-worth gained in the family should help to prepare people to enter the nonfamily world and to find there a further basis for attaining a deeper form of self-respect. Under the morality of authority, the child's perspective is revised in a way that allows the child, as he matures, to understand the way the nonfamily setting is organized to contribute to his self-worth. Thus, as children mature and enter school and build relationships outside the home, they develop an ability to think from the standpoint of others who are a part of their common social orbit. In a well-ordered society, persons learn to "take up their (others') point of view and to see things from their perspective."[12] To do this, people must develop "the intellectual skills required to regard things from a variety of points of view and to think of these together as aspects of one system of cooperation."[13]

In the morality of association stage, people come to understand how more complex social settings than the family can still be cooperative undertakings, governed by a common end to which the entire structure of roles is organized to contribute. "In due course a person works out a conception of the whole system of cooperation that defines the association and the ends it serves."[14] People recognize that the larger social setting beyond the family requires and expects that in return for the benefits they receive, they must maintain certain obligations.[15] People learn to honor these obligations, and they manifest the skills required for doing so in order to gain respect from others.[16] As a part of the morality of association each knows that there are others "out there" who value (or who show respect for) their lives by sustaining the structure of the social organization and in doing so, promote the development of persons.[17] In this setting, people develop toward other associates a sense of fellow feeling and they establish the basis for mutual respect and cooperation, for friendship, and for the concomitant virtues like trust, fidelity, integrity, and impartiality.[18]

From this account it is clear that a strong desire to help one's fellows counterbalances the tendencies to focus only upon obligations to parents, and indeed this morality of association teaches one to interpret love for parents in a way that does not interfere with a strong sense of commitment to aid other association members. But fellowship and friendship could themselves be overly narrowing experiences from the standpoint of the quest to create a morality of principles if they led to a mentality in which one only accepted as legitimate the interests, perspectives, and goals of those associations one was a member of. In this case other associations could be viewed with indifference, if not hostility. Rawls would not wish to see morality turn in a direction solely of group loyalties but he wishes citizens to uphold principles of justice that protect group diversity and provide chances for diverse forms of individual flourishing. Rawls, in describing his centerpiece vision of a social union of social unions, hopes for just institutions that allow citizens to realize a "common aim of cooperating together to realize their own and another's nature in ways allowed by the principles of justice."[19] Further, Rawls says,

> It helps to show that the primary concern is that there are many types of social unions and from the perspective of political justice we are not to try to rank them in value. . . . A well-ordered society, and indeed most societies, will contain countless social unions of many different kinds.[20]

To affirm as a major value in one's life the concept of a society containing diverse groups that facilitate different conceptions of self-respect (the social unions of social unions), one must not locate one's moral outlook on society just in one's family or in one's own group. The moral outlook must encompass the diversity of associations, recognizing and valuing the contributions each makes to the society while also valuing how the preservation of rights and liberties protects this whole.[21]

This more general or enlarged perspective rests upon acceptance of the assumption that society must be a "fair system of social cooperation between free and equal persons."[22] For Rawls, fairness is an "overarching fundamental intuitive idea, within which other basic intuitive ideas are systematically connected."[23] The elements of a fair system are the following: (1) cooperation is not a "socially coordinated activity [and organized] by some central authority," but it is a system of rules that "those cooperating accept"; (2) cooperation is to be reciprocal and mutual: "all who are engaged in cooperation and who do their part as the rules and procedures require are to benefit in some appropriate way as assessed by a suitable benchmark of cooperation"; (3) the idea of cooperation presumes that members of the society have some conception of their own good, which the scheme provides them with an opportunity to achieve.[24]

Fairness is a pivotal intuitive ideal that points citizens toward embracing the society for its basic commitment to being a cooperative arrangement that facilitates diverse notions of self-development. But fairness cannot be fully comprehended in these terms except if citizens can envision the meaning of fairness in the context of its actual unfolding in the society as a whole. To attain this understanding, it is necessary to have an enlarged view that allows one to look upon the society from a perspective that would enable one to understand the diverse nature of society and to determine if the various sectors and roles actually make possible a form of cooperation which secures the development of persons. In other terms, the enlarged viewpoint which seeks a fair, cooperative society is premised upon an answer to a critical question. As citizens look upon society from an enlarged view, they ask if there is in fact substance to the concept of fairness. Here the question is whether a society that says it provides rights and liberties in order to secure a cooperative setting that makes possible diverse forms of self-respect actually lives up to its claims.

In summary, Rawls's morality of principles, as I have interpreted it here, makes sense only if it is associated with a critically reflective posture of citizens which is driven by an expectation that, to use the language of chapter 5, the society is not just formally legitimate, but that it is substantively legitimate, too. Formal legitimacy means that the society must clearly define what the basic rights mean, and then accord them to all citizens. But a morality of principles signifies as well that as a consequence of providing rights to all, society has become a fair, cooperative arrangement that hastens the development of persons. And by making as a primary issue the question of whether or not society in practice lives up to this ideal of fairness, or substantive legitimacy, citizens manifest a morality of principles in their actual conduct. Once again, the morality of principles, just as the moralities of authority and association, is grounded in an enlarged point of view. But the enlarged viewpoints of the moralities of authority and association are limited to a particular social setting that is designed to aid only the members of that setting. In the morality of principles, the enlarged point of view encompasses all particular family and nonfamily settings in a way that seeks a full integration or a basic arrangement of the society that uses rights and liberties to secure the development of all persons.

IV. PUBLIC REASON AND THE DISCOURSE OF FAIRNESS

The commitment to maintain a fair, cooperative setting can best be understood by what would appear to be an inevitable conflict for the ideal citizen in a liberal society, the conflict between the desire for fairness within society and the reality that at times society falls short of the mark. This conflict, and the discourse of fairness which resolves it, can be best understood by explaining the nature of Rawls's moral persons.

In Rawls's theory moral persons would, as a consequence of their sense of justice (or commitment to his principles of justice), revise and reformulate their own life plans when the latter clashed with the constraints embodied in the just social institutions of the society. Here citizens manifest the importance in their own life of the priority of justice. In the Dewey Lectures Rawls characterizes rational persons as moral persons with two important moral powers.

> The first power is the capacity for an effective sense of justice, that is, the capacity to understand, to apply and to act from (and not merely in accordance with) the principles of justice. The second moral power is the capacity to form, to revise, and rationally to pursue a

conception of the good. Corresponding to the moral powers, moral persons are said to be moved by two highest-order interests to realize and exercise these powers.[25]

Individuals have the capacity to define their own good, and under the second moral power, they do so in terms of their own personal choices for life. The second moral power by itself is not the main feature of the moral personality. However, when it (the second moral power) is joined to a firm commitment to the principles of justice (the first moral power), the goal structure of the person reflects a desire to pursue basic goods only in conjunction with an equally strong desire to conform one's conduct to the principles of justice.

For Rawls, given that persons have a moral capacity, it then is the case that they can and will accept the fact that major political and social institutions are governed by rules of justice. In pursuing their interests persons will conform their conduct to the rules of just institutions. The real test of this moral capacity is how well it stands up to the conflicts which are inevitable features of even a well-ordered society. In particular, it is possible that the very same institutions that secure self-respect for some may harm others, and a mature form of enlarged thinking would recognize this possibility. But committed to upholding the views of society as a cooperative entity that is based on rights and liberties provided to all, persons would seek ways to overcome the problems they witness. And they would do so initially by taking seriously the claims they hear from others that the social scheme harms them. By taking the point of view of those who make such claims, the concern is not how to gain advantage over them, but how to gain a full understanding of their claims, so that people can fairly judge their validity. As enlarged thinkers, people would then seek to compare their claims and arguments to those offered by others, and from this activity try to derive an opinion as to each claim's validity. As Rawls says, persons in a well-ordered society approach matters of conflict by acting "to take up the point of view of others, not simply with the aim of working out what they will and probably do, but for the purpose of striking a reasonable balance between competing claims."[26] If the claim involves a question of rights and liberties for all, citizens in this culture, because they are committed to securing them from a sense of principle, have a "common allegiance to justice [and this fact] provides a unified perspective from which they can adjudicate their differences."[27]

Often this type of discourse centers upon how to remove the barriers to full social and political equality. Once society provides to each member rights in the formal sense, it is clear that to fully take advantage of them and thus to use them to enhance one's development, the social barriers that stand in the way of one's using them for this purpose must be removed. Thus, where barriers to employment and education exist, for instance, citizens lack the resources needed to make full use of their basic rights and liberties. What is the use of having freedom of speech or participation if as a result of a lack of education, one has not learned how to form opinions through public reasoning or how to participate effectively on their behalf? What is the sense of having the right of private property if one is excluded by various social barriers from full participation in the economic life of the society?

To remove the social barriers that prevent society from becoming a cooperative setting for all citizens, it is necessary that the discussion of policy issues within the government be predicated on the objective of using public reason to achieve fairness. In particular, in the discourse of fairness, public officials must examine the claims of those who allege harms done to them by the society. When persons allege that owing to the nature of particular social policies there are barriers to their participation in the society, and thus to their use of rights to promote their self-development, then it is necessary to assess these claims, and if they are found valid, to use the power of the state to find remedies that remove the harm.

In conclusion, a citizen-state relationship grounded in the discourse of fairness is a society where citizens are influenced by the discourse of fairness to understand and to appreciate the various contributions others must make to maintain society as a cooperative setting. But just as important, they understand also that the social arrangement must at times be modified to include within the cooperative setting those not fully covered by it. If it were the case that public officials abandoned the attempt to frame their deliberations in terms of a concern to secure fairness for all, then the worth and importance of basic rights and liberties, as well as the just cooperative setting they contribute to, would be considerably diminished. The practical impact of this action would be to make the rights and liberties appear to lose significance, and in this event the essence of a liberal state would be destroyed. For in the absence of the discourse of fairness, rights and liberties would no longer symbolize a cooperative setting that tried to benefit all, but instead would symbolize a cooperative setting that provided privileges only for some.

An enlarged understanding, in its form of public reason dedicated to fairness, is critical at both the political and social levels to protect a just, cooperative ethos in society. In the next chapter, we discuss the political will that must prevail in order for an enlarged culture and its discourse of fairness to continue.

V. RAWLS AND THE CHARGE OF CORPORATISM

The question in this section is whether Rawls's theory resists corporatist tendencies. Some writers, like Stephen Esquith and Richard Peterson, say Rawls's theory does not.[28] I disagree with them, and in this section, I provide the basis for my position.

For Rawls, a just political system or a system committed to securing basic rights and liberties is a "case of imperfect procedural justice."[29] This means that while procedures are constructed to attain just ends, the procedures themselves are not always likely to do so. "The characteristic mark of imperfect procedural justice is that while there is an independent criterion for the correct outcome, there is no feasible procedure which is sure to lead to it."[30] The imperfect character of the political process signifies that the political system of a democratic society is a "regulated rivalry." Here "political power rapidly accumulates and becomes unequal; and making use of the coercive apparatus of the state and its law, those who gain the advantage can often assure themselves of a favored position."[31] Indeed, the advantaged will seek to arrange the social environment to suit their own designs, and as a result, they may have no concern for the needs of others. Even if they do have concern for the needs of others, they may still make decisions that inadvertently harm those whom they seek to aid. In this view, then, politics, even in a liberal society committed to democratic principles, always stands on the verge of creating a corporatist relationship between the state and many of its citizens. Rawls is not an advocate of this relationship, and he points out that, for instance, even institutions like universal suffrage may not be a sufficient means to avoid it, and he leaves the general problem of how to avoid dangerous concentrations of power to political sociology. Here, Rawls argues that he is only interested in defining, in his discussion of politics, an ideal political arrangement, which can be used to judge actual institutions.[32]

Esquith and Peterson argue that Rawls's conception of the original position necessitates his acceptance of a corporatist relationship between the state and its citizens. Their argument rests on the conception of society that is made central in Rawls's original position. In the view of society provided there, Rawls, who may desire not to support a corporatist setting, ends up doing so nonetheless. And this setting excludes any possibility of basing public policy on what I have labeled the discourse of fairness.

I argue here that Rawls's original position neither necessitates a corporatist relationship between the state and its citizens nor rules out the prospects for a discourse of fairness, a discourse that combats this relationship. The discourse of the original position seeks a social organization that requires people to follow certain rules of conduct, rules that when followed allow citizens to pursue their own life plans. Esquith and Peterson derive from this fact the notion that society inevitably is designed to support a corporatist form, and this way of life would not make as a central element to policy-making the discourse of fairness. But in fact even within the original position Rawls conceives of citizens assessing the worth of the results of the procedures of an ideal arrangement, and because of this, the notion of a discourse of fairness is not ruled out. And because it is not, then the corporatist environment is not a necessary result of the original position. In the discussion that follows, I hope to develop this argument in greater detail.

As is well known, in Rawls's original position persons determine the nature of the basic principles of justice behind a "veil of ignorance." This means that persons seeking to determine the basic structure of the just society, which is the basic objective of the original position, are excluded in this hypothetical situation from knowing their particular place in the social order. Thus, persons do not know their interests or particular needs. Citizens do have a general understanding of the way society works. "They understand political affairs and the principles of economic theory; they know the basis of social organization and the laws of human psychology."[33] In particular, they know that there will be different levels of accomplishment in society based on differences in the possession of basic goods, talents, and opportunities. Society will be organized in a manner that gives some greater access to the attainment of their life plans than others.[34] Still, in the original position it is assumed that it is rational for each person to always seek a larger share of the basic goods that provide access to his life plans.[35] Moreover, it is also assumed that some will do better than others, and overall there will be a worst off position, wherein people at the bottom of the society have the least amount of income and wealth. Citizens not knowing their particular place in society and not wanting to fall into the lowest rung would decide to support a principle that both assures basic liberties to all (and thus to themselves) and requires the better off to be willing to contribute to enhance the fortunes of the worst off. This "conservative" attitude reflects a form of rational self-interest; if one ends up at the bottom, one hopes that the bottom is a decent place to reside.[36] Here people would support the provision of basic liberties to all in a setting where the better off contributed to secure decent life chances for the least well off.

The discourse of the original position is not in the main accommodationist. Since no one knows "his situation in society nor his natural assets . . . no one is in a position to tailor principles to his advantage."[37] Consequently, the parties have "no basis for bargaining in the usual sense."[38] Instead, because no one knows his own situation, it is presumed that each is similarly situated and thus would be "convinced by the same arguments."[39] "If anyone after due reflection prefers a conception of justice to another, then they all do, and a unanimous agreement can be reached."[40] The approach to finding common principles is not one wherein people holding different views of shared principles or even different principles must find a way to accommodate their differences. The discourse of the original position signifies that what one person finds as an acceptable conception of justice, all others would as well, on the basis of the same reasons.

The central conclusion Esquith and Peterson draw from the original position is the commitment that evolves to make a set of just procedures the basis for attaining the goals just described. Thus Esquith and Peterson point out that the original position leads to support for making a notion of pure procedural justice the basis for social interaction, and this in turn rules out any form of public reason in the manner of a discourse of fairness as the basis for political life. Esquith and Peterson argue that people in the original position would opt for a set of just procedures whose results are always reasonable,[41] or what Rawls calls always just.[42] Esquith and Peterson equate the just procedures with the notion of a free market. "He [Rawls] accepts the notion of a freely working market mechanism and, moreover, one with an outcome whose justice is guaranteed so long as its internal rules are followed."[43] Here, "the market is an instance of pure procedure insofar as it is capable of determining a definite outcome, and it does so according to rules whose observance is sufficient guarantee of the legitimacy of this outcome, whatever it may be."[44]

Indeed, Rawls, in discussing the pure procedure, outlines the background of the just basic structure, and the latter maintains Rawls's principles of justice (see footnote 1) by a law and government which is to "act effectively to keep markets competitive, resources fully employed, property and wealth . . . widely distributed by the appropriate forms of taxation, or whatever, and to guarantee a reasonable social minimum."[45] Rawls also assumes that a just basic structure would provide equality of opportunity through universal education and that this structure would also secure all other liberties. For Rawls, this system, which permits the establishment by the government of a social minimum at an appropriate level, should create just results in the distribution of basic income and wealth so that the difference principle, or the idea that the better off improve the condition of the least well off, is secured too. But for Esquith and Peterson, when politics is designed to protect the market, it puts into place a state that in the name of protecting the market actually protects powerful interests, thereby sustaining a corporatist setting. These groups deny nonmembers a chance for participation in policy-making; indeed, powerful groups work through administrative agencies they control both to make policy and to administer it by keeping nonmembers from participating in either process. Legislators elected by the citizens cannot make the law in keeping with a commitment to protect the full participation of all citizens, nor can executives elected by the citizens do anything but protect the most powerful. In this setting, the public officials erect a state that appears to act as a neutral mediator among conflicting groups in order to secure the free market, but this appearance only "obfucates"[46] the fact that the state is not socially neutral and that it is not even democratic.[47] But citizens who believe otherwise hold fast to a myth, and the original position in Rawls really is an effort, certainly an unintentional one, of course, to perpetuate this myth. Thus Rawls is a "second-order ideologist" whose "procedural politics may then be said to mediate class conflict, but it is class conflict bent through the prism of the complex network of bureaucratic capitalism."[48]

However, Esquith and Peterson fail to address the fact that citizens in formulating principles in the original position, manifest a distrust, if not a fear of the corporatist mode. And they realize that the market may not produce results that always prevent this form from emerging. This understanding puts citizens in a position of needing to rely upon a political system which allows them to intervene and break down those corporatist formations that threaten the principles of justice. Given this understanding, then, it is once again both possible and necessary that citizens engage in a discourse that allows them to judge the fairness of the society and that is the basis for effective action on behalf of their judgments.

In making the argument for this claim, it must be clear that Rawls opts for a democratic conception of the distribution of basic goods instead of a liberal one. The latter is seen as correcting the distribution based on natural liberty, which in supporting the view that careers be open to talents presumes a free market economy and rights and liberties for all. Here, the distribution is designed to provide certain persons, who possess natural talents and abilities, with greater amounts of wealth and income. Moreover, because there is no attempt to preserve "an equality, or similarity of social conditions" (except for the provision of similar liberties for all in a free market setting), the existing distribution of wealth is determined by prior patterns of natural assets. Social circumstances would favor only those persons and talents favored in the prior distribution, unfairly excluding others with talent. The liberal interpretation says that careers should be open to talent *and* that everyone should have a fair equality of opportunity to attain careers befitting their talents. Prior distributions of wealth cannot preclude the development of all persons of ability. Still, just as in the natural liberty view, the liberal interpretation would distribute opportunities on what Rawls sees as an arbitrary criterion, the "natural distribution of abilities and talents."[49]

Under the democratic conception, however, individuals are provided the same liberties, and those who succeed in the system must contribute to the least well-off members. "The intuitive idea is that the social order is not to establish and secure the more attractive prospects of those better off unless doing so is to the advantage of the less fortunate."[50] Thus in discussing the second part of the second principle of justice — that social and economic inequalities are to be arranged so that they are attached to positions and offices open to all, the principle of fair equality of opportunity[51] — Rawls is clear that this principle is lexically subordinate to the difference principle or to the idea that the distribution of basic goods should be to everyone's advantage.[52]

It is clear, then, that Rawls's citizens even in the original position would not always put trust in the free market as Esquith and Peterson contend. For the free market might permit a form of distribution that gave superior benefits to a few without their having to contribute to the overall well-being of others. Unequal distribution is acceptable only if it is to everyone's advantage.[53] Thus Rawls discusses the importance of the need for a "general point of view" from which to judge the social system and to determine whether the social and economic inequalities that result from the market process are satisfactory. Here Rawls discusses the importance of the representative man. The latter first specifies that each person is to have the same rights and liberties guaranteed to all members of the society. The market process cannot interfere with this principle. Second, the representative man is a statement of the acceptable level of basic income and wealth that persons in each social category, including especially the least well off, should possess.[54] In introducing the representative man, Rawls suggests that pure procedures, or as in this case the market process, may not always in fact produce the just results promised by reliance on pure procedures, and thus there needs to be a standard to determine the justness of market results. Rawls says that if the society accepts free trade, one must accept the results even if "specific interests suffer."[55] This suggests the view held by Esquith and Peterson that Rawls approaches the market uncritically. But Rawls says that "this [acceptance of free trade] does not mean, of course, that the rigors of free trade should be allowed to go unchecked. But the arrangements for softening them are to be considered from an appropriately general perspective,"[56] which is that of the representative man.

In making necessary an evaluative standard, the door is left open for a political system that allows citizens to assess the justice of the distribution of basic liberties and wealth produced through a market process. Citizens will seek from the political process redress from harms done to them by the economic process, and they will use as their defense the claim that society has not properly lived up to the standard of the representative man. Here, citizens in one social position might argue that the conception of the representative man for their position has not been adequately realized in practice. Or they might claim that the conception of the representative man itself is inadequate for their social position. Indeed, citizens might argue for a new method to define the representative man for each social position. When claims of these types are made by citizens in one social position, then, citizens in other social positions stand to have their fortunes affected if as a result of a claim the conception of the representative man is changed for any level of society. Especially, it is the case that citizens who are at the least well-off place may expect to be affected more severely than other citizens at higher social positions.

The process of the free market cannot resolve disputes of this sort; only citizens engaged in a discourse of fairness can. Rawls's original position clearly points to a need for the discourse of fairness even if the original position does not move to devise one for society. Still, Rawls's original position, in providing a democratic conception of equality, can be viewed as removing any corporatist obstacle to this kind of discourse. For in a democratic conception of equality, citizens are always given to understand that they can judge the results of the social and economic system to ensure that it meets the standards of justice that all accept. But if corporatist power relations were allowed to dominate, this option would be denied to ordinary citizens. Rawls's political system must facilitate the discourse of fairness that the original position makes a possibility. Otherwise citizens would always have to abide blindly by the results of a market process, and then they would lose an ability to be critically reflective citizens, able to act effectively upon their judgments. Does Rawls's political system afford citizens this opportunity? Esquith and Peterson argue that Rawls's four-stage political process excludes this possibility.[57] I argue otherwise.

The four-stage process starts with a constitution that defines the basic rules for making and enacting policies, rules that preserve basic liberties. The legislature, acting with a general knowledge of social facts, would seek to make policies regarding social and economic issues having to do with "maximizing the long-term expectations of the least advantaged under conditions of fair equality of opportunity, subject to the equal liberties being maintained."[58] The legislators do not define the rights and liberties; these have been defined already by the constitutional convention, but the legislator is to make general policies that protect these liberties and preserve the principle of fair equality of opportunity. In doing so, the legislators do not have specific information about their own situation; they have only general information about the way the society is structured.[59] This is necessary to ensure impartial application of the shared principles of justice. In the last two stages, administrators and citizens do in fact know the specific situations of citizens. The former apply the laws to specific circumstances, and the latter are affected by the result.

In this view of politics, citizens with a particular agenda go to the level of government most able to provide for their needs. If they seek general legislation pertaining to occupational safety, for instance, citizens address the legislature. If citizens seek application of an existing occupational safety law to a particular case, they ask for help from the appropriate administrative body charged with enforcing the law. In the first instance, the legislature reacts to claims from the standpoint of the general socioeconomic trends in society and asks if there are classes of people, including the least well off, whose basic liberties or whose fair equality of opportunity is affected negatively by an existing social situation. In the second instance, the administrator understands the factual substance of a claim and tries to determine how a general law should be applied in a particular case.

When politics is conceived solely in this fashion, deliberation in the form of a discourse of fairness could be threatened. The placement of decisional power in different functional agencies truncates the political process to such an extent that it is impossible to fully consider the claims of those who say the system harms them in some manner. In this situation, it is possible for the legislature to make laws that others administer, but at the same time have no oversight authority over those who administer these laws. And yet, part of the claim of unfairness might evolve from those citizens who argue that the administrative agency charged with carrying out a law does so in an unjust manner. In this case, citizens, not being able to challenge the legislature to change the administrative agency's behavior, would have no recourse but to appeal to the administrative agency and convince its members to work to their advantage. Thus, Esquith and Peterson say, "Deliberation and debate give way to pressure group activities and bureaucratic wheedling. Citizens acquire a new rational competence: the ability to recognize where in the policymaking process their problem belongs and to which functional branch of government they should argue their case. They recognize when they have to hire a lawyer, enlist a lobbyist, consult a pollster, or recruit expert testimony."[60]

In this case, the power of certain administrative agencies would grow, and the ability of these agencies to stand in an autonomous relationship to the legislature would increase. The legislative branch that makes the law could not be ensured that the law was enforced in the manner they intended. Nor could the legislature consider this question by itself as it developed laws. Citizens might claim that an administrative agency had treated them unjustly and that the law should be reformed to reflect this fact. But if the administrative agency is autonomous, this concern is beyond the scope of the legislature. This fact in itself makes impossible as a basis for politics a form of public reason based upon a discourse of fairness. For this discourse cannot take place unless the legislature can listen to and consider all claims, including those that the administrative agencies are acting unjustly. Further, the legislature must have the authority and power to affect changes in the administrative structure; otherwise, the discourse of fairness will be perceived as lacking any political effectiveness.

If the four-step process led to the outcome Esquith and Peterson describe, then a corporatist outcome would be inevitable. But there is no basis for arguing that Rawls rules out and excludes the idea that the legislators can and should oversee the actions of those who administer the general laws legislatures make. This view derives from the fact that legislators in Rawls's ideal scheme would not be denied the prerogative to consider particular claims from citizens that the social system harms them. As legislators sought to secure both the basic liberties and fair equality of opportunity for all, including the least well off, they could look at particular citizen claims from the standpoint of whether or not they symbolized broad social patterns that if left unchecked would undermine these goals. The debate could include a discussion of the claim that certain administrative actions threatened the basic liberties and fair equality of opportunity of certain members of society and that the administrative context needed reform. Indeed, the claim could be made that the administration of certain laws had led to a general betrayal of the commitment to the provision of basic rights and liberties for all. And to turn this pattern around, it could be mandated that the legislature pass laws that constrain administrative agencies in certain ways.

In discussing these matters, the full gamut of points of view on the question of the protection of basic liberties and fair equality of opportunity would have to be considered and ultimately accommodated. In doing so, there is no reason to presume that a discourse of fairness, one which sought to achieve agreement among diverse interests, could not and would not take place in Rawls's constitutional process. The different views could be tested and a consensus could emerge that some would accept and others would still reject. But the latter could in this setting continue to mount their argument, if in fact they still believed strongly in their cause. Rawls's political institutions, which are modeled on the liberal regime's commitment to representative politics, need not exclude the possibility.[61] And Rawls never says they do. Thus the prospect of collective deliberation, and in particular what I have termed the discourse of fairness, is not denied a central place by Rawls's political system. The only question, then, is where in Rawls does this discourse evolve from.

The point is that if the discourse of fairness is not excluded in the original position, it is not encouraged either. The concept of the original position does not encourage the discourse of fairness because it is mainly concerned to define the basic structure of society. It is not designed to demonstrate how citizens discuss particular claims in the context of just institutions. Still, as already argued, Rawls suggests that citizens would in fact always be concerned with evaluating the results of just institutions. And since the original position does not rule out an enlarged discourse as a means to do so, then it is clear that this discourse is not excluded in Rawls's society. As long as it exists, corporatist forms are put in jeopardy. Finally, as we have shown, the discourse of fairness fully emerges in the social learning process, and it is here that collective deliberation of society can be nurtured so that the political process is located in a full commitment to achieve fairness and rights in a substantive sense.

8

The Political Will
of an Enlarged Culture

I. INTRODUCTION

The experience of an enlarged culture will not by itself guarantee its perpetuation. Large differences in opportunity or basic material goods could lead society into a state of class warfare, and this would certainly threaten an enlarged culture. Ideal liberal citizens understand that the cornerstone of their politics is a public policy that does not permit inequalities to threaten an enlarged culture and the critically reflective citizen body that the enlarged culture promotes. In making this claim, I point to the work of Michael Walzer's *Spheres of Justice*.

II. THE SHARED UNDERSTANDINGS IN WALZER'S SPHERES

For Walzer the basic character of a society is that it is a place where citizens share common goods and values. Human society is a "distributive community" of a variety of goods that people need.[1] He says there is no single principle of distribution: "There has never been a single criterion or single set of interconnected criteria, for all distributions."[2] Goods are distributed in various spheres of domains defined by a set of values, held in common, that describe the nature of the good distributed and the way in which it should be distributed. Because these goods are understood to be distributed in a variety of life contexts, the basis for their distribution in one sphere cannot be the basis for distributing a different set of goods in another sphere. "Every social good or set of goods constitutes, as it were, a distributive sphere within which only certain criteria and arrangements are appropriate." Further, Walzer says, "there are standards (roughly knowable even when they are also controversial) for every social good and every distributive sphere in every particular society; and these standards are often violated, the goods usurped, the sphere invaded, by powerful men and women."[3]

Despite the frequent violation of these spheres, society still considers it to be unjust for a person who has been successful in one sphere to attempt to use his influence to override distributive principles in another. For instance, persons who accumulate a great deal of wealth (legitimately within the sphere of money) should not have greater influence in the political sphere as a result of their wealth. Nor should they "buy and sell others," or have greater likelihood of achieving political office, and so on.[4] The integrity or, as Walzer says, "autonomy" of the spheres must be maintained if the shared values of a pluralistic order are to prevail.

This view of sphere integrity has several important implications. First, Walzer's account of justice is, as he says, local, and therefore "justice is relative to social meanings."[5] In constructing a view of justice that is situational, it might appear that Walzer wants only to provide a concept of justice that is uncritical of whatever distribution takes place. But that is not Walzer's intent. He argues that in the shared understandings there is a kind of "latent" social vision that moves the society to a more egalitarian structure. Walzer says. "it [equality] is a practical possibility here and now, latent already . . . in our shared understandings of social goods. *Our* shared understandings: the vision is relevant to the social world in which it is developed; it is not relevant . . . to all social worlds."[6] For Walzer an egalitarian vision is said to be implicit in the shared understandings: "If such [an egalitarian society] isn't here—hidden, as it were, in our concepts and categories—we will never know it concretely or realize it in fact." In the same place Walzer says that our culture moves constantly toward egalitarianism, and thus our concepts "tend steadily to proscribe the use of things for purposes of domination."[7]

It would seem that there are two ways to understand the implications of this vision. In the first instance, the rules for distribution of goods relevant to each sphere must be applied equally to all persons. Persons may disagree about the nature of these rules, but once formed, these rules must be applied uniformly. Thus, in the modern setting if the rule is to ensure a certain level of welfare, then all members of the sphere are entitled to that level of welfare.

In the second instance, Walzer's concept of equality within his spheres seems to refer to the question of the nature of the rules of distribution. Here the spheres embody actual rules that are used to distribute necessary, basic goods. I concentrate on this aspect of equality in this chapter, and my argument is that in a liberal society the rules must permit a decent minimum that provides necessary, basic goods in sufficient amounts so that each person can have a dignified life, with a reasonable chance to pursue his own conception of his life. A decent life, however, will not eliminate arguments concerning the "better" or "best" distribution of basic goods on behalf of achieving a more humane or fair social order. These arguments about the fairness of the distributive system will be ongoing, with society's commitments shifting in the direction of one view of the "better" or "best" distribution and then to another. But society can tolerate this ambiguity as long as the distribution rules distribute basic goods in a manner that makes possible a decent life and thereby avoids the emergence of deep social antagonisms that undermine an enlarged culture, one which manifests public reason and a discourse of fairness.

III. THE CONFLICTS WITHIN THE SPHERES

Walzer discusses a variety of spheres: citizenship, social welfare, education, money, office, leisure, love, hard work, religion, political power, and recognition. I cannot discuss all of them here. I will discuss only a few of these spheres and point out the public controversies that pertain to them.

The major spheres are citizenship and social welfare. Citizenship pertains to the question of which persons should be allowed to be recipients of all the basic rights and liberties as well as fundamental material goods and opportunities. This issue is always controversial, especially as it is raised with regard to aliens who apply for citizenship.[8] In deciding who to admit and who not to, immigration questions are always matters of "political decision."[9] Thus one can ask if it is just for people who flee to this country from Central America or Haiti to be sent back. For some, these people should not be returned to a dictatorship to suffer amidst poverty; for others, these aliens would be nothing more than drains on the local economies where they come to reside and to require public services. The reason these matters are politically controversial is suggested in the latter response.

In granting citizenship status to others, the society agrees to include new members under the protections granted to all citizens. For once a new class of people is included in the citizen category, they cannot be denied basic rights and liberties as well as a basic distribution of material opportunities and goods, and this fact means that the existing citizen body must make good on its new commitments to new citizens. For many existing citizens, extension of these commitments constitutes added burdens that, when weighed against other important priorities, should not be undertaken.

Contained in this view of citizenship is the understanding that society as a cooperative arrangement secures the elements of survival and general decency, or what is called social welfare and security. Indeed, societies are formed in part in response to the need to provide those basic goods that individuals need to survive decently, but that individuals cannot supply by themselves. "Men and women come together because they literally cannot live apart. . . . Their survival and their well-being require a common effort."[10] In a liberal society the nature of the particular shared understanding that defines the notion of social welfare and security presumes an agreement in accordance with what Walzer understands to be three principles. He says that "every political community must attend to the needs of its members as they collectively understand those needs; that the goods that are distributed must be distributed in proportion to need; and that the distribution must recognize and uphold the underlying equality of membership."[11]

Walzer understands that his three principles "apply to the citizens of the United States; and they have considerable force here because of the affluence of the community and the expansive understanding of individual need."[12] Still, for Walzer, the United States has one of the "shabbier systems of communal provision in the western world."[13] This view of the American system of welfare can be understood in one of two ways. In the first way, the major problem is that the American society does not provide enough to secure even a decent minimum to its members. For instance, Walzer says that in the area of legal aid, money should be spent in proportion to need. But not enough is provided to the poor to ensure equal justice for them. The rich and the poor are subject to different treatment in the court system because there are not enough funds provided to the poor to ensure that they are treated, as the courts require, in the same way as the rich. "If justice is to be provided at all, it must be provided equally for all accused citizens without regard to their wealth."[14] And consequently a decent minimum must be made available to the poor to make equality before the law possible.

In the second way of approaching welfare issues, the system does provide enough for a decent life, but some argue that it could and it should do better. For instance, take the case of medical care. In this area there seems to be a minimum standard that provides for the poor access to free clinics, and in this setting the poor are assured of basic care. Walzer finds this standard inadequate, but not necessarily unjust, since presumably the clinic system would provide decent care. But he says that Americans, given their "common appreciation of the importance of medical care" have gone even beyond this standard to provide a better system.[15] Walzer points out that federal, state, and local governments subsidize different levels of care of different "classes of citizens." Just how far the society should go in giving better care is the subject of much public debate. Walzer hopes for a better or more enhanced standard, one that takes into account the public support for research, hospitals, and advanced medical care, and he says that "as long as communal funds are spent [for these things]," the benefits of these advances should be made available to everyone.[16] But in suggesting this, he demonstrates the view that it is not always enough to secure a decent minimum, but, at least with regard to medical care, there is a better standard that must be used, and he believes that the general public agrees on the need to search for one and to put it into place. Here, in the example of medical care, the concern in distributing basic goods is not only to provide more people with these goods, but to provide more people with access to better goods.

In this discourse, the subject for debate is the nature of a fully humane society. The question is, Why not provide more than just the basic minimum for a decent life? For instance, in the area of education, which includes provision of publicly supported grade school and high school training, why not secure for each a chance for free education to whatever level is needed to cultivate particular talents and skills? In the area of welfare programs, which ensure basic allotments of food and other necessities, why not provide a guaranteed annual income which permits citizens of all social classes to enjoy a certain amount of security in their lives? In the area of medical care, why not ensure, in addition to providing basic aid for ordinary diseases or ailments, a chance to have those kinds of services only the upper middle class and upper class in income can have, like psychiatry, elective surgery to enhance one's appearance, and so on? In the area of the criminal justice system, which provides court-appointed attorneys for the indigent, why not permit each citizen the chance to be able to finance the lawyer of one's choice, just as the very wealthy may do? These are all concerns which are at the heart of the basic question: Is society fully humane?

In these as in all the other spheres Walzer discusses, there are serious disagreements. Moreover, the problem is made even more perplexing because the lack of agreement that is typical in a liberal society is probably more sharply pronounced than Walzer is willing to recognize. In each of the spheres mentioned, there are major conflicts over the nature of society itself. Should society promote community values in its distribution rules or should it promote individualist ones? In other terms, should society be conceived as a set of institutions facilitating individual life plans and denying the impact on people of a communal good, which if imposed, would threaten individual freedom? Or should society be organized to achieve shared, collective goals, in which case each person would be expected to transform himself or herself into a communal self committed to promoting shared goals?

Each conflict about the "better" or "best" distribution, if seen from one or the other point of view, would symbolize not just a difference of opinion that temporarily stood in the way of consensus, but a difference of ideology which (given our cultural limitations) would make a permanent and enduring consensus perpetually elusive. As is often the case, liberal societies seek to accommodate both views, but in doing so, there are constant political swings in which on some occasions for some issues, society appears to take a more individualist approach and later for the same issue it adopts a more communalist approach, with the possibility of a further swing back to individualist approaches in the future. For example, take the problem of how to provide a "better" form of social welfare. At times, some may promote the growth of the welfare state on the grounds that the society should see itself as a community with each member willing to enhance, through increased taxes, the chances of the worst-off members not only by providing basic resources for a decent life, but by expanding them to include more of the benefits of an affluent society, including most importantly a chance for a free education as far as one's motivation and abilities take one. Yet there are strong pressures (which are dominant today) for swings in the other direction, too. Here the concern is that welfare state activity should grow only if people who are recipients of its benefits are willing to work and contribute to the fund that helps to provide them. Otherwise, in this view, people are made dependent on a system that robs them of their autonomy and self-respect. In addition, unless the recipients of state benefits work, those who do provide these benefits by their work may consider that the social system is not a fair, cooperative arrangement and that it undermines respect for individual effort and thus minimizes the importance of diversity. These attitudes have led to calls for a work requirement for all who receive state aid.

Despite these policy shifts and the continuing disagreement they reflect, it is still the case that we can speak of "spheres of justice," or the existence of shared values and understandings that undergird the political process and sustain a pluralist world anchored in respect for diversity. But how is this possible? In other terms, given the many political disagreements of a liberal society pertaining to the "better" or "best" distribution of goods, why doesn't society break down into opposing, irreconcilable groups undermining the shared under-standings and common values pertaining to things like citizenship and the need for social welfare?

The first and most usual answer is that because government acts from publicly accepted rules for resolving conflicts, the results of the process are acceptable. Here we presume that where the citizens in a given sphere cannot themselves resolve a conflict, publicly sanctioned governments (at the local or national level, depending on the scope and nature of a conflict) operating by acceptable rules, are the best place to turn. But if the sense of social solidarity were based com-pletely on the shared expectation that governments have rules to work out solutions to conflicts (over the distribution of basic goods), given the fact that such conflicts persist even after the conflict resolution attempt sanctioned by government, then citizens might question the worth of the entire political system. People might contend that the practice of the government does not conform to the expectations per-sons have of it, and thus withdraw their respect for the government and the shared values of the community. The practice of the political institutions would by itself not be the basis for securing a sense of social solidarity.

What contributes to respect for the political system is when it can sustain an enlarged citizen-state relationship through the discourse of fairness. The latter is designed to assess the validity of the claims made by those alleging that the social arrangements harm them. Public officials and citizens must address these claims with an intent to determine their validity. In the discourse of fairness, different views must be considered by each party to the discourse. The discourse con-tributes to political stability because in considering diverse views on how best to maintain a shared value, let's say as in this case, welfare, it becomes clear to all that the society is committed to protecting this common value, despite the disagreements that arise over how best to do so. The same goes for the discussions of how best to achieve other shared understandings: In attempting to determine, as the discourse on fairness requires, a consensus on the "better" or "best" way to embody these values in policy, the commitment to these values is reaffirmed by each of the diverse elements of society.

Moreover, the understanding of why these values, as well as the regime which adheres to them, are important in the first place is also reaffirmed. That is, as diverse people with different understandings approach through an enlarged discourse the question of how best to achieve the society's shared values, then it is clear that these values are meaningful as shared values because they symbolize a commitment to sustain diversity. Here, as a result of the practice of an enlarged discourse based on the commitment to fairness, both strains of the liberal culture, individualism and communalism, are protected. A regime that is based on this possibility is one to which citizens will have a strong obligation.

Conversely, without an enlarged culture, when people disagreed about how best to promote shared values, they would read into this disagreement either a desire on the part of some to destroy the shared values or a desire to sustain them but to exclude certain citizens, without good reason, from coverage by them. Therefore, what helps to maintain the enlarged culture itself becomes a matter of great importance to nurturing political stability in a liberal society. I contend that an enlarged culture is itself dependent upon a firm understanding of and commitment to providing those basic goods which secure a decent life for all persons, and I wish to develop this point further in the next section.

IV. THE NEED FOR SOCIAL MINIMUMS

The discussion by Robert Thigpen and Lyle Downing on Walzer's argument is instructive in this regard. In discussing Walzer's concern for providing medical care to all who need it (in contrast to the existing practice, which Walzer condemns), Thigpen and Downing argue that implicit in Walzer's argument is the notion that "fellow citizens agree that when goods are publicly funded they should be available to all in proportion to need."[17] This presumption of an implicit standard in the culture can be used to critique existing practice. Thigpen and Downing can then go on to argue that the "way to gain distance from unreflective opinion about shared understandings is to focus directly on the common life as a standard by which to judge belief and practice."[18] Citizens can find these values when they ask themselves, "What must citizens provide to one another if they are to have an inclusive common life?"[19] In the matter of medical care, the answer would be distribution according to need. Given this approach, "Walzer could argue that something as important as medical care should be provided in proportion to need, assuming that it could be provided without seriously curtailing the provision of other vital needs."[20]

The common standard, in this case for medical care, represents an important aspect of the spheres of justice. For liberal society to survive there must be a basic commitment to a minimum level of material decency. This is the case precisely for the reason that equality is not so much a "latent" shared understanding as Walzer claims, but an explicit expectation in liberal society that citizens have a right to demand be fulfilled. Therefore where citizens understand that one of the values of a society committed to the development of persons is that all persons are to have this opportunity, then when this goal is thwarted citizens will believe that the spheres are designed to provide a decent life for some and not for others. The effect of this understanding is to lead people, especially those harmed by the distribution of basic goods, to believe that there are rules for distributing basic goods in ways that secure a decent minimum, but that these rules are not uniformly applied to all persons. This conclusion might be acceptable in a society that lacks an explicit commitment to equality, but in a society where that commitment exists and where it means that public goods are to be provided at a level necessary to secure decent life chances for all, when this principle is violated people will believe that a basic article of faith has been broken and in response bitterness and deep social antagonisms will arise. Further, if it appears the society fails in this regard, then the individualist-communalist conflict will easily be turned into intense social antagonisms. In this setting an enlarged culture will not thrive; in fact, it will not be able to exist.

When the enlarged culture breaks down, then an ideology resistant to respect for equality emerges as a central outlook. Liberal societies like the United States have a long history of various forms of bigotry: sexual, racial, religious, and regional. All forms of bigotry contain the same fear of diversity and all of them argue that certain types of life should not be tolerated. This attitude suggests that social policy should be made with an intent of denying to the targets of bigotry the same goods and liberties all citizens are entitled to have. When these values become entrenched, they further deepen the social antagonisms, justifying the view that certain citizens can be denied basic rights and goods, even if in doing so society acts to contradict the shared understanding that a citizen by virtue of being a citizen cannot be denied basic rights and goods.[21]

The existence of bigotry in a liberal society like the United States indicates that this society may at times reflect the side of its history that stands in opposition to equality. But from the standpoint of the argument made here, it is also true that sexual bigotry, racism, religious prejudice, and regionalism have been resisted and if not driven from this country's liberal culture, reduced in importance. Yet it is still true that these attitudes pervade this society in such a potentially strong way that at any time that an enlarged culture is weakened, these attitudes may well reemerge to regain their former prominence. If they do, then all past efforts to reduce their impact will have been for naught. Therefore, to combat these attitudes it is necessary to maintain an enlarged culture, but to do this, there must be a continuing commitment to provide basic goods on a basis that ensures decency. For if these basic goods cannot be distributed in a manner that avoids intense resentments and antagonisms, then the enlarged culture suffers breakdown, and the attitudes hostile to equality, always close at hand owing to our history, will be used to destroy the liberal commitment to support basic rights and liberties for all citizens.

In effect, then, because the maintenance of an enlarged culture depends on the provision of basic goods, it is necessary to argue that basic goods such as medical care, education, and welfare are to be accorded to people for the same reason other basic liberties such as speech and conscience are provided as a basic right. Thus even if the argument about the consensual principle that defines the "better" or "best" distribution continues, still, as long as basic goods are in fact provided and guaranteed at a level to secure a decent life, then citizens will avoid a situation where the individualist-communalist schism moves toward becoming a form of intense class antagonism. The latter undermines the enlarged culture and opens the door to the reaffirmation of historical attitudes hostile to securing the basic character of a liberal regime and its commitment to basic rights and liberties.

It is true that liberals in this country have often made much of their commitment to provide basic goods from what they argue is a compassionate concern for the cause of the poor. But it is just as true that this gesture has often appeared to be disingenuous. In response, liberals may claim that the failure to achieve this goal rests upon finding the right mechanism for delivering it, and not from a lack of compassion on their part. Perhaps the various programs that have been suggested since Lyndon Johnson's Great Society have had their flaws, but the intentions behind them have been clear: to demonstrate compassion for the have-nots and to enhance their life chances.

Whether or not these programs need to be replaced is an open question that will not be addressed here. But in a society where the importance of an enlarged culture is clearly understood, then the political will must exist to make sure that material dignity for all who are citizens is *the* major item on the public agenda. Citizens will then realize that as they discuss how to allocate social resources, the key question, the one that must addressed first, is how to provide material dignity to all citizens.

But this concern becomes of minor importance in a society where the protection of an enlarged culture is deemed to be unimportant. There is a suspicion that this may well be the fate of modern liberalism. The fact is that if the public culture of enlarged thinking is not valued as highly as it should be, then citizens, and especially policymakers, are less intent on making the provision of basic goods the main item on their domestic agenda. Without this sincere and intense commitment, these goods are not provided, the social system begins to manifest the signs of deep social antagonisms, enlarged thinking becomes less important and central, bigotry reappears in our politics, and these factors, taken together, undermine respect for the basic character of a liberal regime.

V. CONCLUSION

The ultimate success of an enlarged discourse comes when it achieves some agreement on what constitutes the "better" or the "best" distribution of certain basic goods. In doing so, the so-called "better" distribution then is viewed as a necessary basic good that must be provided to secure a decent life to all citizens. Indeed, if this "better" or "best" distribution is not provided, then it is possible that the enlarged discourse itself will be placed in jeopardy. It is always the case, then, that the standards for the nature of what constitutes a decent distribution of basic goods may well be elevated over time as a result of the discourse of fairness. What yesterday was a matter of contest and disagreement, today is understood as a necessary basic good that must be provided to all.

For instance, whereas at one time it was argued that social welfare needs should all be handled through private charity, today the state is understood as having a fundamental role in providing many basic and necessary goods. Medical care is a prime example of this point.

In a former era, doctors were to provide free assistance to the needy. Then, as it became clear that this approach was not sufficient to provide adequate care, local and state governments became involved in supplying it, initially through public clinics and publicly funded hospitals. Now, as the question of basic health care for the needy is investigated further, it is possible that future discussions will consider expanding the medicaid program for the needy to the point where the latter are entitled to the same quality medical care open to the financially best off members of society.

Progress is marked for the society as it moves in its enlarged discourse do settle issues consigned to the "better" or "best" category regarding particular types of goods. Once settled, a new standard for what constitutes a necessary distribution of a basic good is established, and society must maintain it if the enlarged discourse is to continue. Then society can move on to discussions of other goods as it tries to resolve the "better" or "best" distribution for them, too.

9

The Surrounding Conversation
of Liberal Societies

I. SUMMARY

To summarize the general argument, the liberal regime is predicated upon a basic commitment to provide basic rights and liberties to all citizens in order to secure the self-respect and development of all persons who fall within its purview. In addition, a liberal regime reflects a commitment to constitutional government and to the need to maintain society as a cooperative arrangement that citizens voluntarily accept. In the former instance, the notion of a liberal regime is associated with a governmental form which divides power among three branches (executive, legislative, and judicial), and in achieving balance, no single agency of government is allowed to dominate the policy-making or policy-implementing processes. As a consequence, the inevitable corruption that accompanies power must not be allowed to undermine the quest to attain policies that reflect a consensus of the members of the society.

According to the need to maintain society as a cooperative association among the members, society is an association that exists by common agreement. Of course, people inherit the society they are born into, and thus it is not the case that they have a chance to give their formal consent to its constitution or to particular laws the state makes. Yet even if the state affords citizens no basis upon which to give their formal and direct acceptance of the state, still, as long as the state supports policies citizens accept, then citizens live in a society they *could* give their consent to, if given a formal way to do so. And in fact citizens symbolize their giving or their refusing to give consent

131

through the methods they choose to protest state policies they do disagree with. This mode of giving consent is indirect and informal. Thus, if they choose, within the challenge tradition of a liberal regime, civil forms of protest that do not threaten the state's authority and ability to rule within its constitution, then citizens demonstrate by the respect they show authority their support for maintaining the state and thus their strong sense of obligation to it.

In protecting rights and liberties and constitutional balance, the liberal state seeks to avoid a corporatist form. Here, powerful interests arise and set up an autonomous base of power within the government and then proceed to make policies and enforce rules, while excluding all other interests from participation in the policy process. The modern liberal society is always threatened with this outcome. As we have argued, the contemporary liberal state has created administrative agencies designed to oversee and run programs in a variety of areas. There are agencies to administer programs in agriculture, defense, welfare and a myriad of other areas. The key constituency groups for these programs may successfully gain a dominance in the policy-making and policy-implementation processes through these agencies. When they do, they try to dictate the outcome of legislative delibera-tions as well as executive branch actions. The courts may even become powerless to stop them, and in this way, a few control a policy area in a way that eliminates the participation of other interests in the policy process. Here, constitutional balance is overturned and replaced by a corporatist relationship between the state and its citizens. In this case, citizens who are excluded may feel justified in protesting through noncivil means, and this statement of one's weak sense of obligation to the state's authority is likely to be interpreted by the state as a threat to the state's ability to govern and as the symbol of an intent by citizens engaged in noncivil conduct to informally withdraw consent to its rule.

Most importantly, noncivil citizen protests of corporatist rule sym-bolize a demise of the underlying cultural experience that is suitable to the needs of the critically reflective citizen and that is associated with constitutional balance and a cooperative setting in a liberal soci-ety. When there is constitutional balance and when efforts are made to maintain society as a cooperative setting, the expectation for liberal citizens is that liberal society will not be characterized just by its pro-tection of rights and liberties, but also by its commitment to maintain the enveloping enlarged discourse. Here, citizens and policymakers both understand that political judgments are made through an effort to find an accommodation among diverse views, as people holding similar principles seek an agreement on how best to implement them. The culture shares a commitment to liberty, equality, rule of law, and so on. But there are different understandings about how these principles are to be understood, especially in relation to particular issues. Citizens must narrow their differences and find a way to accommodate them if the principles they share are to continue to be protected. To do so, they must accept the fact that their views and understandings are partial, and to be made whole, they must be tested against the views held by others. In the process, citizens may change or modify their views somewhat out of respect for those held by others. At some point, a formal procedure will be used to test the consensus, usually a vote either among citizens as a whole or among members of a legislative body, and the majority outcome will be binding. Those who disagree will of course seek to continue to discuss the issue at hand in the hopes of getting the public to reconsider it and perhaps pressure the government to do the same. In any event, in this enlarged culture, public officials are committed to maintaining the enlarged discourse of society by resisting the paralysis of corporatism.

In a setting where the politics of a society embody an enlarged discourse, the key issue of policy-making is always fairness. Citizens make claims that the existing structure works against and harms them. The citizens of the society and the policymakers must then fully consider these claims, seeking a way to resolve them in a manner respectful of all the points of view which are a part of the discourse. As citizens attempt to reach an accommodation, they must strain to hear the views they disagree with and make every effort to find a way to include them in the resulting solution. This process helps to protect the real significance of rights and liberties as devices that work to make possible the full development of and self-respect for all persons.

The enlarged discourse can only take place in a society committed to secure fair opportunities and basic material security to all citizens. Otherwise, citizens will believe the policy-making process is used to rig the social structure in a manner that supports the interests of a few against the rest. In this case, the discourse of fairness would fall into a form of strategic speech and action in which one segment of social interests united against another segment and society became a battleground, with the victor measuring success by how solid a corporatist foundation it placed under its commitment to achieve its interests. The discourse of fairness, once replaced by the strategic objective of how to get and keep power to gain advantage, leads to the diminishment of constitutional balance, and in this case society fails to make possible the provision of rights and liberties for the development of and respect for all persons. Here, instead of being given a social learning process that teaches the importance of rights and liberties in a context dominated by enlarged thinking, citizens are taught how to think and act in strategic ways with the intent of denying a place to others in society, even at the cost of fairness and cooperation.

These points serve to demonstrate what is at the heart of the liberal regime, a shared understanding of and commitment to the common values that taken together make up what Rawls calls an "overlapping consensus."[1]

II. THE ADEQUATELY THICK COMMUNITY

For Rawls, the central value consensus of a liberal society, or its "overlapping consensus," is a commitment to rights and liberties for all, the need for "an agreement on guidelines of public enquiry and rules for assessing evidence," and the need for the "cooperative virtues of political life," such as a willingness to compromise and to meet "others halfway."[2] From the standpoint of the argument made throughout this book, each of these principles is important for the reason that they, like the other principles just summarized, may be "signs" of an enlarged culture. This means that given an enlarged culture's central importance to a liberal society, principles like the right to challenge authority, the need for constitutional balance, and a notion of a cooperative society based on fairness are significant values only when they are seen as contributing to an enlarged culture. For without an enlarged culture, these values come to signify a practice that stands in opposition to what these values promise. In the absence of an enlarged culture, the right to challenge authority or constitutional balance, for instance, is only an idea which symbolizes a hope for a free and open society, which cannot in practice be realized. Or in the absence of an enlarged culture, a liberal society fails to achieve a cooperative setting that can search for and realize fairness. Moreover, whereas citizens may value these principles as ideals that all should strive to protect, unless these principles are seen as being able to help make possible an enlarged culture, from the standpoint of practice the culture's shared principles may be viewed as useful only for those who wish to deceive people into believing that a corporatist system of governance should be seen in favorable terms.

Further, in asserting the importance of an overlapping consensus, it must be clear that liberal citizens are being asked to conduct their lives in accordance with the shared principles of the liberal culture.

The liberal community is not so thin (or lacking in a need to have citizens make certain values primary in their lives) that it promotes a form of value relativism. The importance of this point must be underscored. In an enlarged culture citizens must retain their critically evaluative posture toward life. There would be little incentive to do so, however, where the society is simply constructed from a commitment to value relativism, for then all values would be equal in worth, and there would be no need for, indeed there would be no value placed on the critically evaluative citizen.

But in saying that a liberal community requires adherence to the basic ideas and principles just enumerated, it is important to note that adherence in this case does not connote a requirement that citizens adapt their lives to the canons that determine for them just how they should look upon major questions of public policy that would otherwise be controversial in the society. Were society predicated upon acceptance of canons of this sort, then the society would be structured both to produce them and to require adherence to them. A kind of Plato's *Republic* would be the order of the day, with a set of truth sayers standing atop a bureaucracy that imposed the truth onto its citizens. These canons would determine the "better" or "best" distribution of essential goods as well as the best position on the individualist-communalist schism for each issue area where the distinction was relevant. But if a liberal society rested on a value system this "thick", then once again the critically evaluative person could not exist. In this case, the reason is not because all values are equally good, but because only one set of canons should be followed by all, and once those are determined no one has any need or right to question them.

But since public reason takes place in a setting predisposed to protect and to appreciate the individualist-communalist conflict, it cannot be expected to produce a Platonic system of coherent judgments and principles, which themselves become the basis for a liberal society. Today's judgments may be challenged tomorrow, and today's consensus is subject to revision. This fact arises from the understanding that citizens will constantly start their analysis, even as they seek to provide protection for basis rights and liberties, from one or the other of the two strains. Their arguments will also be guided by the knowledge that the opposing strain, which cannot always be accommodated, must still be protected, thus making certain that an enduring consensus will be difficult to find on many issues of public concern. If citizens succeed in this endeavor, they show that their culture is not so thin as to make critical reflection superfluous nor so thick as to make it impossible, but that instead their culture is adequate to sustain the activity of a vibrant and critically reflective culture.

What may threaten an enlarged culture and the overlapping consensus of shared values on which it rests is the general loss of respect for ideas in our society. As Sartori says, liberal regimes depend upon the possibility of an "idea-struck age." Liberal culture is mostly endangered by a "pattern of distrust and suspicion of ideas."[3] Sartori says that there is a tendency to reduce all ideas to ideology. In this event, ideas are seen as merely the products of an existing social order that seeks to maintain itself by reinstilling in people those beliefs that will motivate people to perform as their society requires.[4] From this viewpoint, people do not see ideas as the vehicles for gaining a critical independence in order to criticize constructively their society. Instead, the ideas they hold represent a pattern of life that seems unbreakable, and as a result the notion that they might critique this system and change it seems to be an undertaking both remote and senseless.

But it is quite possible that the loss of an idea-rich culture is really a result of the distortions of a technique-conscious world. In a technique-conscious world, what counts the most is the ability to master the techniques that are the basis for control. Ideas that have importance are those which tell people how to act in certain circumstances to accomplish particular goals. But in an enlarged discussion, the problem is that we lack a precise understanding of how best to proceed, and our objective is to test our ideas against other people's views in the hope of finding out the best course. But still, owing to the individualist-communalist schism, we find that many of the ideas we discuss must be constantly reevaluated in the light of new arguments presented by others. An enlarged culture does not lead to the precision that people in a technique-conscious world demand. As a result, an enlarged culture connotes an experience that defies the effort to reduce thinking to technique, and this fact for many is proof enough of the futility of liberalism.

III. SOCRATES AS THE IDEAL LIBERAL CITIZEN

Finally, there is much discussion today that our education system is in a state of collapse because there is little respect for thinking and even less for ideas.[5] Allan Bloom, fearing this malaise, calls for the restoration of the Socratic model to university life. But one must be careful in following the call. For in this view, Socrates is seen, as in the tradition of Plato, working to create a social and political hierarchy whose sole purpose is to give philosophers the resources to contemplate truth from the standpoint of pure reason. Only a unique few can grasp truth at this level, and so naturally the rest will be placed in a support role for those who can. If successful, philosophers will construct an integrated system of concepts all connected back to the core truths deemed true by pure reason, and this system of truth can be the basis for organizing life to attain its proper purposes. This Socrates is not the philosopher who extolls the virtues of an enlarged culture, but is likely to be its chief critic.

Seen from this standpoint, the Athenians could have argued that Socrates' view of philosophy threatened the culture of democracy. To make this hypothetical argument, I assume that the Athenians would have claimed that they sought to protect the Periclean vision of democracy. Socrates, in the midst of this setting, would be viewed as arguing for the importance and significance of philosophy. To carry out the search for the truth that philosophy seeks, Socrates would find it necessary for the state to support this activity. Principally, this means that Socrates must have the right to free inquiry.

Given the account Plato gives of Socrates' trial, it would appear that free inquiry is what the Athenians hope to deny him.[6] But an argument could be made by them that demonstrates not only that they seek free inquiry as well as what free inquiry supports, democracy, but that they seek to protect it against Socrates, who is the chief threat to it. In this view, the Athenians would have held that the effort to create a system of concepts all tied to a key truth is an impractical approach to making political judgments. Useful judgments can only be made in a setting where the members of the society are willing to accept the enlarged discourse as the foundation for judgment. It is the case that citizens may share common values and principles but disagree on how to apply them in particular instances. To maintain the cohesion of the society, it is necessary to create a culture whose central theme is the need for an accommodationist discourse. In this setting, citizens compare views and modify their own position in relation to the other views they hear. As a result, it is the case that an agreement that leads to a Socratic system for judgment may not arise. The judgments that emerge may even require that citizens tolerate within the same society competing and contradictory moral purposes.

Still, as long as the tradition of enlarged discourse remains, then citizens can work to forge agreements that more nearly approximate a form or way of life that provides fair treatment for all citizens. But Socrates, at least as depicted by Bloom, might resist this argument, and say against it that this point of view represents the perversion of philosophy by democracy. An accommodationist discourse will not make the best argument the basis for action, and then the truth will neither be determined nor made the basis for conduct. But the citizens of Athens could have argued, to the contrary, that in fact Socrates' view of philosophy, because it threatens the enlarged discourse, threatens democracy. For the Athenians if could have been the case that the truth is what emerges from the imperfect, but only, guide to action citizens have, an enlarged discourse. To assume that this is not the proper foundation for action is to pursue a path that does one of two things. First, it may put the rule of the society into the hands of an elite who operate from a myth that they have truth, and in doing this, a few may rule the many, and the concern of the few may not be the good of the many but only the good of the few. Or in the absence of an accommodationist discourse among the citizens, perhaps the only way to settle differences is by a form of coalition politics in which certain groups gain strategic position and place other groups at a permanent disadvantage. This shoving match approach eliminates, as in the case of the rule by a few, any hope for fairness. Thus in each case democracy would be destroyed.

So the Athenians act against Socrates, and they have him put to death. Sadly, their actions may have done even more to threaten democracy than did Socrates' steadfast commitment to philosophy. For the enlarged discourse that undergirds democracy cannot continue if individuals are faced with severe penalties for their opinions. The enlarged discourse presumes the possibility of respect for persons, as we argued earlier in chapter 2, and when respect for persons is denied, so is the enlarged discourse. Thus, in their enthusiasm to protect democracy by securing the form of discourse that makes democracy possible, the Athenians acted against their own interests.

If we continue to assume, in the face of this action, that the Athenians would have claimed to be supporters of free inquiry and democracy, then what should they have done to protect democracy from Socrates' view of philosophy? To counter Socrates' view of philosophy, it would have been better had the Athenians put forth another role model, or a different Socrates, one who saw philosophy as championing the traditions of enlarged thinking. The new, liberal Socrates, would be a man who made his life with the ordinary people and who with them faced practical questions and problems that pertained to the basic fairness of the society. This Socrates, as understood within the context of the argument of this book, would accept the fact that philosophy cannot use pure reason to construct the basis for making practical judgments about fairness and that only enlarged thinking, in the guise of the discourse of fairness, is useful in making political judgments. In a liberal society that protected this standard,

Socrates would work patiently to accommodate the diverse interests and conceptions of the good that permeated the society. This Socrates would be a political moderate, and he would maintain a strong obligation to the state by demonstrating his respect for authority anytime he criticized or protested particular laws he disagreed with.

But where the society rejected the enlarged culture standard, Socrates would easily become a political radical who resorted to protest forms that manifest a weak obligation to the state. This means that he could be motivated by a need to secure the conditions of an enlarged culture and to do so he might choose forms of protest that threatened the state's authority, even if this tactic put at risk basic rights and liberties. It is clear, however, that given the commitment to an enlarged culture, this Socrates, ever ready to be the radical, would prefer to live in a liberal state where his politics could be moderate and his sense of obligation to authority strong. Then, the society would manifest his fondest hope for an arrangement of the basic rights and liberties that worked to preserve an enlarged culture.

IV. CONCLUSION
THE HOPE OF THE LIBERAL STATE

The symbol of Socrates as a defender of the ideal liberal citizen and the enlarged discourse may seem strange to some. Still, the hope of making this kind of discourse the basis for the liberal state is not a foreign idea to liberalism or to its defenders. For instance, Bruce Ackerman seeks to defend the liberal regime by demonstrating that at its heart lies a neutral dialog. The neutral dialog says that "a power structure is illegitimate if it can be justified only through a conversation in which some person (or group) must assert that he is (or they are) the privileged moral authority." This view leads Ackerman to make the principle of neutrality the basis for discourse. This principle asserts that "no reason is a good reason if it requires the power holder to assert: (a) that his conception of the good is better than that asserted by any of his fellow citizens, *or* (b) that, regardless of his conception of the good, he is intrinsically superior to one or more of his fellow citizens."[7]

Ackerman's project rejects as the basis for liberal society a form of discourse that is predicated upon a perfectionist view of the world. But in asserting this point, it is necessary also to accept that there is a natural temptation for citizens to search for ways to make their conception of the good *the* conception of the good. Ackerman's insistence upon a discourse that searches for the acceptable reasons for political judgments, reasons which, in his case, do not imply or require that one find oneself "intrinsically" superior to others, must demonstrate the foundation for citizens finding this approach to discourse desirable and necessary. Not only does Ackerman's project depend on this possibility, but the liberal regime hinges on it too.

Often however, both defenders of the liberal state and critics (of the liberal regime) with liberal sentiments, overlook this important requirement. This happens when in the name of promoting a basis for moral and political discourse, one seeks a perfect form of communalism or individualism by attacking the view one objects to. In the process, what is overlooked is why an enlarged culture becomes so central to the liberal regime. In particular, a liberal culture contains both strains, and to secure each in a manner that makes possible the protection of rights and liberties as well as an authentic rendering of both strains, it is necessary to respect the traditions that speak to the importance of limits on both. And further, what facilitates this possibility is, in the liberal culture, an enlarged discourse.

Ackerman himself seems only partially to understand the importance of this point. This fact is best demonstrated when in order to protect the neutrality principle against other forms of justification, especially his rendering of the social contract view and utilitarianism, he fails to put the cultural flesh on the bare bones of his argument for a neutral dialog. He argues that his view of neutral dialog grounds citizens in actual social settings, and not in "some transcendent individual who may sit as higher judge of our social conflicts."[8] Liberal approaches to judgment always involve an "appeal to a hypothetical being who transcends the social situation in fundamental ways. It is this formal characteristic that lies at the root of the traditional dilemma: once it is conceded that the views of a higher judge are relevant, the only way to win an argument is to claim that one's view of the higher judge is somehow better than that of one's antagonist."[9]

But the real world, says Ackerman, is lived at the level of people with competing goals and interest conflicts "settled in some organized way."[10] Symbolizing this day-to-day conflict is the tension between the individual and the community. On the side of the individual stands the contract theory view that "demands that the political community respect the claims of self-interested individuals."[11] On the side of community stands the utilitarian who sees individualist striving to attain private happiness as a danger to the public good, and so the utilitarian "rightly insists that no individual promote his self-interest into the public interest without taking others' self-interest into account."[12] Thus "the utilitarian must be trained to view himself in an unbiased way—as just another sentient member of the political community."[13] In each case, "the two sides go wrong only when they try to promote their half-truth into a whole truth."[14] Moreover, each side conceives of individuals in terms that attack their individuality. Writers in the tradition of the contract theory use such abstract terms to define the nature of individuals that people lose their distinctiveness, and utilitarians provide a view of community that also denies the distinctiveness of persons.[15]

It is the virtue of Ackerman's view of discourse that people are not to lose their particularity as an effort is made to "construct a truly liberal relationship between individual and community."[16] Clearly, this is a chief benefit of public discourse. But to be successful in this project, it is necessary to demonstrate the nature of the traditions which make possible and desirable a discourse that can in fact provide the bridge between individual and community. Ackerman seems so intent on telling us how critical a public discourse is to a liberal society that he neglects the additional task of demonstrating further the elements of the actual social context that help to make both possible and desirable a discourse-based society.

What justifies the public discourse of liberal society are the cultural understandings that make this discourse an integral and thus accepted part of liberal society. In particular, citizens who think that their view of the world is better than others' still may realize the need to temper that view in debating policy, in order to avoid the dangers associated with holding their views in the extreme. As I argued in chapter 3, this fear of the extreme is a real fear that can motivate ideal liberal citizens to understand that the good one supports may be undermined unless one is willing to approach its realization through an attempt to accommodate it to the view of the good held by others. Indeed, it is this understanding that makes an enlarged culture a matter of central importance, for the enlarged culture provides a way to accept limits without threatening the character of the strain one supports or undermining the basic rights and liberties of a liberal regime. Because the enlarged culture is so important, it must be understood, and to be understood, its nature must be carefully delineated by liberal citizens. This is necessary so that citizens can understand the essence of what they must work to maintain. To this end, Kant and Smith have been helpful in clarifying the liberal project. The enlarged culture, with its commitment to public reason and to fairness, is built upon the rules of commonsense understanding found in Kant as well as moral sentiment of sympathy embodied in Smith's impartial spectator.

Given the importance of an enlarged culture to a liberal society, then, the task for liberal citizens is clear: It is one of defending the traditions that make an enlarged discourse possible. Kantian rules of understanding and Smith's neutral spectator can survive in a society where the expectation of citizens is that its major political institutions are to create an enlarged relationship to its citizens. Constitutional balance, the challenge tradition, rights in the formal and substantive senses, a social learning process—these practices can survive in a way that secures the liberal state if they help make possible the enlarged discourse that liberal cultures thrive upon.

To make the protection of the traditions of liberal discourse the foundation of a liberal society means, in conclusion, that defenders and critics of liberal regimes must not allow themselves to lose sight of what makes possible a search for fairness among competing conceptions of the good. If this course is followed, then those committed to protect an authentic liberalism can strive politically to make the cultural setting of an enlarged discourse possible, and truly, as a result, a common and fundamental good all can support will be protected and nurtured.

Notes

CHAPTER 1

1. A. John Simmons, *Moral Principles and Political Obligations*, (Princeton University Press: Princeton, N.J., 1979), p. 192.

2. In the view taken here, however, the state seeks to protect its authority, and where citizens have no obligation to authority, the state will do so even at the cost of threatening rights and liberties. Indeed, even Simmons suggests this conclusion, albeit indirectly. He says that citizens "have natural duties to do may of the things normally required by law." To secure citizen adherence to their duties, however, the state may have to become coercive. "In short, then, much less disobedience by citizens and much more coercion by government can be justified within the terms of the anarchist conclusion than might at first appear" (A. John Simmons, "The Anarchist Position: A Reply to Klosko and Senor," *Philosophy and Public Affairs* 16:3 [Summer 1987], p. 279). In this view it is possible that the state, to preserve the natural duties citizens owe one another, will have to act with extreme coercion, even denying basic rights in order to secure natural duties. Certainly Simmons would not find this a happy moment, but it is moment implied by his view nonetheless.

3. Giovanni Sartori, *The Theory of Democracy Revisited*, vol. 2, (Chatham House: Chatham, N.J., 1987), pp. 302–06. I accept the view from Sartori that political liberty "protects and permits the individual to choose; and the successive freedoms all add sustaining conditions

to greater and more effective choice" (pp. 305–06). I accept that these public liberties permit freedom of choice, including private choice, but in addition, I emphasize that the public liberties give citizens independence from the state in order to challenge its decisions. I emphasize the aspect of independence since I am writing from the standpoint of the ideal liberal citizen, who seeks to be critically evaluative toward state policies. Sartori further points out that this concept of political liberty is best protected in a liberal political regime. It is the latter which establishes methods of constitutionalism for ensuring that there is the rule of law and not the rule of man. (I discuss this aspect in chapter 5.) In particular, the procedures for making and enforcing laws, as defined by the constitutional process, are designed to avoid abuse of authority. Political liberty is what is protected by this process, and this includes the liberties mentioned in chapter 1 and 2. These liberties secure a basis for citizen independence. It is these liberties, then, that become of central importance, and constitutionalism must protect them in a liberal regime.

4. The emphasis on making political liberty of such fundamental importance is central to leading liberal arguments, found most especially in John Rawls's *A Theory of Justice* (Harvard University Press: Cambridge, 1971).

5. Michael Walzer, *Obligations: Essays on Disobedience, War, and Citizenship* (Simon and Schuster: New York, 1970), p. xiii.

6. Joseph Raz, *The Morality of Freedom* (Clarendon Press: Oxford, England, 1986). On this point my argument generally agrees with Raz when he says that it is a "melodramatic exaggeration to suppose that every breach of law endangers, by however small a degree, the survival of the government, or law and order" (p. 102). Here Raz has in mind when he says "government" just institutions, or what I would call institutions that protect basic rights and liberties for all.

7. For a good treatment of the principle of fairness, see Richard J. Arneson, "The Principle of Fairness and Free-Rider Problems," *Ethics* 92 (July 1982), p. 616. Rawls discusses the principle of fairness in *A Theory of Justice*, pp. 108–14.

8. Rawls, *Theory of Justice*, pp. 111–12.

9. Ibid., p. 113.

10. George Klosko, "Presumptive Benefit, Fairness, and Political Obligation," *Philosophy and Public Affairs* 16:3 (Summer 1987), p. 244.

11. Ibid., p. 249.

12. Ibid., p. 249.

13. I am grateful to Larry Biskowski of the University of Minnesota for this point.

14. This argument for a de facto form of consent is an interpretation for how to construe Locke's notion of tacit consent. See John Locke, *Second Treatise on Civil Government*, edited by Thomas P. Peardon (Bobbs-Merrill: Indianapolis, 1952), p. 43, par. 75; p. 68, par. 119.

15. *Theory of Justice*, p. 336.

16. Ibid., p. 337.

17. Ibid., pp. 337, 344.

18. Ibid., p. 114.

19. Ibid., p. 337.

20. Ibid., p. 337.

21. Ibid., p. 338.

22. Ibid., pp. 115–116.

23. Ibid., p. 339.

24. Ibid., p. 340.

25. Ibid., p. 372. Generally, even in defining conscientious refusal, Rawls discusses the case of refusing to take part in acts of war. He indicates that "the refusal to take part in all war under any conditions is an unworldly view" (p. 382). Conscription is "permissible only if it is demanded for the defense of liberty itself" (p. 380). Once again, there is a proclivity to say that when duties conflict, a citizen has a higher duty to the state if the state is just or if it provides basic rights and liberties to all.

26. A. D. M. Walker, "Political Obligation and the Argument from Gratitude," *Philosophy and Public Affairs* 17:3 (Summer 1988), p. 193.

27. Ibid., p. 193.

28. Ibid., p. 200.

29. Ibid., p. 200.

30. Ibid., p. 202.

31. Ibid., p. 202.

32. Ibid., p. 202.

33. Ibid., p. 205.

34. Ibid., p. 206.

35. Ibid., p. 207.

36. Ibid., p. 201.

37. Ibid., p. 201.

38. Ibid., p. 201.

CHAPTER 2

1. Here, I accept the view of Hannah Pitkin, as discussed in chapter 4, that a legitimate state is one to which citizens "ought" to consent. This means that the state and its officials have basic political values which the citizens likewise share. But a legitimate liberal state that secures rights and liberties may not be sufficient to justify a strong obligation, unless it can secure at the same time and enlarged culture. See her "Obligation and Consent," in *Philosophy, Politics, and Society,* fourth series, edited by Peter Laslett, W. G. Runciman, Quentin Skinner Barnes and Noble: New York, 1972), p. 62.

2. Rawls, *Theory of Justice*: Richard E. Flathman, *The Philosophy and Politics of Freedom* (University of Chicago Press: Chicago, 1987); Ronald Dworkin, *Taking Rights Seriously* (Harvard University Press: Cambridge, 1977); Alan Gewirth, *Reason and Morality* (University of Chicago Press: Chicago, 1978).

3. Flathman, *The Philosophy and Politics of Freedom,* p. 299.

4. Rawls, *Theory of Justice,* pp. 60–61, where the argument is made for the supremacy and priority of basic rights and liberties, even prior to the development of the difference principle.

5. Ronald Dworkin, *A Matter of Principle* (Harvard University Press: Cambridge, 1985), p. 408, footnote 1 to chapter 8. Dworkin holds this view of political philosophy and says that the latter "is a structure in which the elements are related more or less systematically, so that very concrete political positions (like the position that income taxes should now be raised or reduced) are the consequences of abstract positions (like the position that large degrees of economic

inequality should be eliminated) that are in turn the consequences of still more abstract positions (like the position that a community should be politically stable) that may be the consequences of more abstract positions still.''

6. Immanual Kant, *Critique of Pure Reason*, translated by F. Max Muller (Anchor: New York, 1966), pp. 385–86.

7. Ibid., p. 386.

8. My argument for a discourse dimension in Kant is indebted to the work of Hannah Arendt, *Lectures on Kant's Political Philosophy* edited by Ronald Beiner (University of Chicago Press: Chicago, 1982), pp. 19, 26–27 and Onora O'Neill in "The Public Use of Reason," *Political Theory* 14:4 (November 1986). The position I develop here places an importance on the possibility of active citizenship. I realize that the thrust of Kant's political thought is against this view, and to make the case, I must argue as Arendt for the political philosophy Kant could have written if he had made the arguments about enlarged thinking in *The Critique of Judgment* central to his politics. For a view that demonstrates the view that Kant would have rejected an active citizen role, see Jean Bethke Elshtain, "Kant, Politics and Persons: The Implication of His Moral Philosophy," *Polity* 14:2 (Winter, 1981). She shows that Kant's citizen would be "an obedient subject" able to participate in narrow and formal types of political practices as a means to manifest their preferences, such as through voting (p. 218). This would make it impossible for citizens to challenge authority (p. 218). Here people relinquish to others the power to make judgments about political matters. Conformity to external rules is the main political requirement (p. 220).

9. Kant, "Metaphysical Foundations of Morals" in *The Philosophy of Kant*, ed. Carl J. Friedrich, (Modern Library: New York, 1949), p. 170.

10. Kant, *Critique of Practical Reason*, trans. Lewis White Beck (Bobbs-Merrill: Indianapolis, 1956), p. 72.

11. Kant, "Metaphysical Foundations of Morals," p. 178.

12. Kant, "The Metaphysical Principles of Virtue," in *Ethical Philosophy*, trans. James W. Ellington, (Hackett Publishing Company: Indianapolis, 1983), pp. 90–91; 108; 116–17. For a discussion of the categorical command to treat others as ends, see Kant, "Metaphysical Foundations of Morals," pp. 170–187.

13. Kant, *The Metaphysical Elements of Justice*, translated by John Ladd (Bobbs-Merrill: Indianapolis, 1965), p. 13. See Kant, "Perpetual Peace," in Kant *On History*, edited by Lewis White Beck (Bobbs-Merrill: Indianapolis, 1963), p. 128. Here Kant says that "all politics must bend its knee before the right."

14. Kant, *Metaphysical Elements of Justice*, p. 13.

15. Kant, "Idea for a Universal History," in *On History*, p. 18.

16. Patrick Riley, *Kant's Political Philosophy* (Rowman and Littlefield: Totowa, N.J., 1983) p. 98.

17. Kant, *Metaphysical Elements of Justice*, p. 35.

18. Ibid., p. 36.

19. Riley, *Kant's Political Philosophy*, pp. 9, 12, 14.

20. Kant, *Metaphysical Elements of Justice*, pp. 82–83.

21. Ibid., p. 82.

22. Riley, *Kant's Political Philosophy*, p. 84.

23. Ronald Beiner, *Political Judgment* (University of Chicago Press: Chicago, 1983), p. 69.

24. For examples of this point, see Kant, *Metaphysical Elements of Justice* pp. 54–60, for private property. Here Kant says the latter is justified by the rule that a "thing is externally mine if it is such that any prevention of my use of it would constitute an injury to me even if it is not in my possession" (pp. 55–56). Further, in discussing public welfare Kant says that "it follows from the nature of the state that the government is authorized to require the wealthy to provide the means of sustenance to those who are unable to provide the most necessary needs of nature by themselves" (p. 93). In discussing punishment, Kant says that the law "concerning punishment is a categorical imperative, and woe to him who rummages around in the winding paths of a theory of happiness looking for some advantage to be gained by releasing the criminal from punishment" (p. 100). He says further, once again in the form of a moral command, "If . . . he has committed a murder he must die" (p. 102). In matters pertaining to the state's right to send citizens to war, Kant says that a "citizen must always be regarded as a colegislative member of the state . . . and as such he must give his free consent through his representatives, not only to waging of war in general, but also to any particular declaration of war" (p. 118). Finally, concerning the rights of states during a war,

Kant says that wars must be fought by principles that will permit states to abandon the state of nature and enter into "a juridical condition" (p. 120). These rules have for Kant universal form, and they fit into a system that supports respect for states that secure respect for persons.

25. John Christian Laursen, "The Subversive Kant: The Vocabulary of 'Public' and 'Publicity'," *Political Theory* 14:4 (November 1986), p. 596.

26. Kant, "Perpetual Peace," in *On History*, p. 129–30. On this general point, once again, it is clear that Kant hopes for a politics informed by morality. The moral politician seeks for policies that establish "harmony" (p. 133). This harmony is possible only in a world with republican governments, with each of them subject to international law that seeks to maintain peace as the basis for the freedom of all the states (p. 133). Here, finally, a coherent system is attained between morality and politics, 'as politics bends its knee to morality,' or in this case publicity (p. 134).

27. Laursen, "The Subversive Kant," p. 596.

28. Ibid., p. 596.

29. O'Neill, "The Public Use of Reason," 526–27. Kant's thought is open to this approach because he himself recognizes that pure reason creates contradictions of its own, and this suggests that an integrated system as the basis for judgment is not realistic. This is the implication, for instance, of Kant's view that pure reason postulates both that men are free and that they are determined (Kant, *Critique of Pure Reason*, pp. 318–19). It should be clear that owing to the antinomies created by pure reason the thrust of reason is to find coherence and to overcome the contradictions that reason itself creates. See ibid., pp. 450–53.

30. Kant, *Critique of Judgement*, trans. J. H. Bernard, (Hafner Press: New York, 1951), hereafter referred to as *The Third Critique*.

31. Ibid., p. 15.

32. Ibid., p. 15.

33. The other type of reflective judgment is teleological. There are two types. One is used to understand history, and it depicts history as if it were designed to achieve a society in which citizens live by the moral law (Kant. *The Third Critique*, pp. 279–284). The other teleological judgment is used in discussing nature, and it sees nature

as designed as a self-sustaining mechanism (ibid., pp. 258–64).

34. Ibid., p. 139.

35. Ibid., pp. 50–51.

36. Ibid., p. 136.

37. Ibid., pp. 136–37

38. Ibid., pp. 136–37

39. Ibid., p. 137.

40. Ibid., p. 137.

41. Ibid., p. 136.

42. Ibid., p. 136.

43. O'Neill, "The Public Use of Reason" p. 541.

44. Ibid., p. 541.

45. Ibid., pp. 541–42

46. Ibid., p. 544.

47. Adam Smith, *The Theory of Moral Sentiments* (Liberty Classics: Indianapolis, 1976), p. 49.

48. Ibid., p. 48.

49. Ibid., p. 162.

50. Ibid., p. 161.

51. Ibid., pp. 162–63.

52. Ibid., p. 232.

53. Ibid., p. 233.

54. Ibid., p. 233.

55. Ibid., p. 67.

56. Ibid., p. 67.

57. Ibid., pp. 67–68.

58. Ibid., p. 140.

59. Ibid., p. 162.

60. Ibid., p. 52.

61. Ibid., p. 166.

CHAPTER 3

1. Dworkin, *A Matter of Principle*, chapter entitled "Why Liberals Should Care about Equality," p. 205.

2. Robert Nozick, *Anarchy, State, and Utopia* (Basic Books: New York, 1974), p. 49.

3. Ibid., p. 50.

4. Ibid., p. 29.

5. Ibid., pp. 109–10.

6. Ibid., p. 33.

7. Ibid., p. 151.

8. Ibid., p. 167.

9. Dworkin, *A Matter of Principle*, "Liberalism," p. 189. In distinguishing individualist liberalism or neutralism from conservatism, for instance, Dworkin is quick to point out that "we cannot say that conservatives value liberty less, as such, more than liberals, [but] we can still say that they value equality less, and that the different political positions may be explained in this way." It is clear, then, that liberals who value liberty in neutralist terms also must value, to secure liberty, some equality.

10. John Rawls, "The Idea of an Overlapping Consensus," *Oxford Journal of Legal Studies* 7:1 (Spring 1987), p. 6.

11. Dworkin, "Why Liberals Should Care about Equality," p. 205.

12. Ibid., p. 205.

13. Ibid., p. 205.

14. Ibid., p. 206.

15. Ibid., pp. 208–09. It should be clear that for Dworkin equality of resources is only a general rule, for which there can be exceptions and "deviations" to promote common shared, public purposes.

16. Ibid., p. 212.

17. John Patrick Diggins, *The Lost Soul of American Politics: Virtue, Self-Interest, and the Foundations of Liberalism* (Basic Books: New York, 1984), p. 67. See also Robert N. Bellah, *The Broken Covenant* (Seabury Press: New York, 1975), p. 27.

18. Diggins, *The Lost Soul of American Politics*, p. 72. Here, the communalist strain reflects a version of the need to live in keeping with a commitment to the public good, but this commitment is not similar in nature to Rousseau's general will because, unlike Rousseau's general will, the American form of communalism does permit the existence of a private realm, and indeed rights and liberties exist to protect this realm against the crushing embrace of an externally imposed "general will."

19. William M. Sullivan, *Reconstructing Public Philosophy* (University of California Press: Berkeley, 1982), p. 180.

20. Ibid., p. 172.

21. Ibid., p. 172.

22. Ibid., p. 173.

23. Ibid., p. 173.

24. Ibid., p. 175.

25. Alasdair MacIntyre, *After Virtue* (University of Notre Dame Press: Notre Dame, Ind., 1981), pp. 50–51, and see p. 207.

26. Sullivan, *Reconstructing Public Philosophy*, p. 175.

27. Ibid., p. 176.

28. Ibid., p. 175.

29. Ibid., p. 168.

30. Ibid., p. 168.

31. MacIntyre, *After Virtue*, p. 215.

32. Sullivan, *Reconstructing Public Philosophy*, p. 175.

33. Michael Sandel, *Liberalism and the Limits of Justice* (Cambridge University Press: Cambridge, England, 1982). He holds a communalist view more in keeping with Dworkin's commitment to equality, and he uses this view in his critique of Rawls. He argues that the problem with liberal writers like Rawls is that they lack a common ground for sustaining a common good, in a kind of society that cannot

really exist without it. Rawls, in arguing for the difference principle, makes the case for the need for the better off to give some of their resources to the worst off, as long as basic liberties are not eroded. But any view of justice that allows a community to make claims on the assets of individuals for the sake of improving the condition of the worst off presumes that persons will allow the "concept of the good" to have priority over the self's choices of what it seeks and who it is. Sandel finds an inconsistency in Rawls's view of persons because for Sandel, Rawls adopts a view of persons that is neutralist, and this view of persons claims a need for independence from a common good. Thus for Rawls, to allow the good "a hand in the constitution of the self" is to "violate the priority of the self over its ends" (p. 149). Similarly, MacIntyre sees the liberal project to have produced emotivism, "which entails the obliteration of any genuine distinction between manipulative and non-manipulative relations" (p. 22). He concludes that "in spite of the efforts of three centuries of moral philosophy and one of sociology, [we still lack] any coherent rationally defensible statement of a liberal individualist point of view" (p. 241).

34. Thus, for instance, those wanting abortion on demand may argue an individualist position, saying that women should have the right of privacy to determine the fate of their own bodies. Those arguing against abortion may use a religious form of the communalist view and claim that abortion violates a basic duty, which is to preserve life in all forms. Still other communalists may claim that abortion is permissible if it is a practice that is sanctioned by the community itself either through existing practices or through the formation of public consensus. And other individualists could claim that abortion is wrong on the basis of a right to privacy, in this case the right of the fetus.

35. William Galston, "Defending Liberalism," *American Political Science Review* 76 (September 1982), p. 627. Galston's position represents an effort to find a substantive foundation for liberalism, a foundation not based just in a procedural formalism. Others are searching in a similar way. For instance, Jack Geise, in "Liberal Political Theory: Reconciling Ideals and Practice," (*Polity* 20 [Winter 1987]), points to Galston as an effort to find a substantive ground in a form of neo-Aristotelean ethical naturalism. Geise accepts the need for providing a substantive ground, but he rejects the neo-Aristotelean view because it is not well enough tied to the anglo-American setting (p. 220). Patrick Neal, in "Liberalism and Neutrality," *Polity* 17:4 (Summer 1985), argues that neutrality cannot be defended as the

essence of liberalism, and as a consequence he suggests a defense based on the question "What does it mean to treat people as equals?" (p. 682). This question requires us to then search for the conditions that will secure this objective (p. 682). Indeed, it is my hope that an enlarged culture will be helpful in this regard. Al Damico, in "Is the Problem with Liberalism How It Thinks?" *Polity* 16:4 (Summer 1984), argues that the political self is a bearer of rights, and thus even if it is unable to "see things from all points of view," (p. 565), the liberal self as a bearer of rights cannot be mired in indifference or even self-interest, but must exercise tolerance. This approach to describing how the liberal self thinks hopes to demonstrate that tolerance is a part of the liberal outlook and thus the liberal self must be concerned with others.

A fear that permeates the current discussion is that a formalist liberalism, especially one that emphasizes an individualist strain, will lead to a paradox in which individuals, seeking freedom, object to all social constraints that may be designed to provide it. See, for instance, Arthur L. Kallenberg and Larry M. Preston, "Liberal Paradox: Self-Interest and Respect for Political Principles," *Polity* 17:2 (Winter 1984), pp. 360–62. In this regard, also see Preston's article on freedom entitled "Individual and Political Freedom," *Polity* 15:1 (Fall 1982). Nancy L. Rosenblum, in *Another Liberalism: Romanticism and the Reconstruction of Liberal Thought* (Harvard University Press: Cambridge, 1987), argues that there is a notion of community implied by the idea of individual freedom. Here she has in mind romantic notions of the individual located in heroic individualism and communitarian visions. Both these visions that emerge from the romantic perspective create the ground for establishing "boundaries between public and private spheres" (p. 188). "In doing this it [romantic liberalism] speaks to the traditionally intractable problem of how to get individuals to take an interest in both public and private affairs. Self-cultivation and self-expression are its distinctive rationales, and individuality is defined as nothing but the way particular men and women go about exploiting the opportunities liberalism provides" (pp. 188–189). Here a particular view of individuals secures its substantive ground. For an important review of this book, see Andrew Sullivan, "Hearts and Rights," *New Republic*, 7 March 1988, pp. 35–38.

36. Galston, "Defending Liberalism," p. 627.

37. Ibid., p. 628.

38. This conception of society as possessing a cooperative social scheme is patterned after Rawls's arguments in *A Theory of Justice*.

What facilitates a cooperative arrangement is an enlarged culture, and how it does this is the subject of the social learning process discussed in Chapter 7.

CHAPTER 4

1. Pitkin, "Obligation and Consent," p. 62.

2. Ibid., p. 63.

3. Ibid., p. 63.

4. Philip Abbott, *The Shotgun Behind the Door: Liberalism and the Problem of Political Obligation* (University of Georgia Press: Athens, 1976), p. 74.

5. Ibid., p. 74.

6. Ibid., p. 74.

7. Ibid., p. 68.

8. Ibid., p. 139.

9. Ibid., p. 67.

10. Ibid., p. 54.

11. Ibid., p. 55.

12. Arthur Kuflik, "The Inalienability of Autonomy," *Philosophy and Public Affairs* 13:4 (Fall 1984), p. 297.

CHAPTER 5

1. Richard Flathman, *The Practice of Political Authority: Authority and the Authoritative*, (The University of Chicago Press: Chicago, 1980), p. 208. In making use of Flathman's views here, some clarification is called for. Flathman's notion of the rule of law is, as he says, "formal in character" (p. 208). But he qualifies this statement by saying that the principles of the rule of law are formal in character, "*comparatively speaking*" (p. 208). This means that he understands that underlying a commitment to the formal dimensions of the rule of law, the commitment to basic rights and liberties, and constitutionalism, there exist "authoritative" values, beliefs, purposes, and objectives (p. 209). In particular, the key value or belief for which constitutionalism works is agency, or the "freedom, rationality and moral integrity of individ-

uals" (p. 186). Flathman condemns the notion of "substantive-purposive" authority because this view suggests a state which imposes its own view of right onto persons, and this is "necessarily unacceptable to anyone with a concern for individual agency" (p. 207). In the use of the term "substantive" in my argument, my intent is to suggest a form of authority that secures a critically evaluative person, a view of persons that Flathman would certainly welcome. But to provide a "substantive" notion of rights, the primary value is not so much agency itself, but what secures agency (as the latter is understood as a critically evaluative person), and what does so is an enlarged citizen-state relationship.

R. E. Ewin, in *Liberty, Community and Justice* (Rowman and Little-field: Totowa, N.J., 1987), argues for a formal proceduralist view as the basis for authority, but he modifies it to secure a substantive notion of rights as I argue for here. He says that obligations are based on whether or not governments follow right procedures. "If the government is corrupt and is not trying to operate the decision-procedures fairly or properly, then the effective procedure by which the decisions are reached is not fair, so the obligations that follow from submission to a fair procedure do not follow in such a case" (p. 114). But he later says that the procedures must signify not just proper application, such as majority rule, but "a fair hearing for the views of each person" (p. 186). Thus, Ewin would seem to support the view of substantive rights provided here.

2. By participatory democracy, I refer to the notions of direct citizen involvement in policy-making as discussed in the work of Carole Pateman, *Participation and Democratic Theory* (Cambridge University Press: New York, 1970), and Benjamin Barber, *Strong Democracy: Participatory Politics for a New Age* (University of California Press: Berkeley, 1984). I will comment on both these writers in the next chapter.

3. Sartori, *Theory of Democracy Revisited*, p. 98.

4. Ibid., p. 98.

5. Ibid., p. 98.

6. Ibid., p. 108.

7. This fact is understood in the language of political science. Elections have meaning in terms of whether they are "critical elections" or not. A critical election is where there is shift from one

majority coalition to another and as a result an electoral realignment takes place. A "maintaining election" is where the majority coalition remains in power. Deviations from a maintaining election can be explained in terms of voter preferences on specific issues or with respect to candidate qualifications. Here the point is that electorates can and do decide policy, as well as decide who should be elected to decide. See, for instance, Peter Woll and Robert H. Binstock, *America's Political System* (Random House: New York, 1984), pp. 232–37.

8. Rawls limits, as indicated in chapter 1, the use of civil disobedience to infringements on his first principle of justice, the principle of equal liberty that says that each person "is to have an equal right to the most extensive basic rights and liberties compatible with a similar liberty for others," and to the principle of fair equality of opportunity, the principle that says the social and economic inequalities are to be arranged so that they are "attached to positions and offices open to all" (*Theory of Justice*, p. 372). Violations of the difference principle, the principle that says that social and economic inequalities are to be arranged so that they are "reasonably expected to be to everyone's advantage," are "more difficult to ascertain" (p. 372), and should be left for a legislative process to decide. Still, if citizens are to be critically reflective in a meaningful sense, the civil challenge tradition cannot be limited in this way. The person engaged in a civil challenge must be able to present their case before public officials and before the public, and it is in this setting that the boundaries of public concern will be defined, as I claim in the last section of this chapter.

9. In developing the notion of public reason, I have made use of Rawls's conception of public reason in his essay "The Idea of an Overlapping Consensus," p. 8. Rawls says that free public reason "needs certain principles of justice for the basic structure to specify its content, it also needs certain guidelines of enquiry and publicly recognized rules of assessing evidence to govern its application." This suggests that the system has certain general principles that must be maintained if the system is to continue to maintain its legitimacy. Rawls says that without public forms of verification there is no "agreed way for determining whether those principles are satisfied, and for settling what they require of particular institutions, or in particular situations. Agreement on a conception of justice is worthless — not an effective agreement at all — without agreement on these further matters."

CHAPTER 6

1. Sartori, *Theory of Democracy Revisited*, p. 245.

2. Rawls, *Theory of Justice*, p. 221.

3. Ibid., p. 225.

4. Ibid., p. 225.

5. Ibid., p. 225.

6. Ibid., pp. 224–25.

7. Ibid., pp. 225–226.

8. Ibid., p. 227.

9. Ibid., p. 228.

10. For instance, see Philip Green, *Retrieving Democracy: In Search of Civic Equality* (Rowman and Allanheld: Totowa, N.J., 1985), pp. 259–66; Barber, *Strong Democracy*, pp. 267–307; Richard Norman, *Free and Equal* (Oxford University Press: Cambridge, England, 1987) chapter 3; Pateman, *Participation and Democratic Theory*, chapter 4.

11. Pateman, *The Problem of Political Obligation: A Critical Analysis of Liberal Theory* (John Wiley: New York, 1979), p. 12.

12. Ibid., p. 18.

13. Barber, *Strong Democracy*, p. 219.

14. Ibid., p. 153.

15. Ibid., p. 145.

16. Pateman, "Political Obligation and Conceptual Analysis," in *Philosophy, Politics, and Society*, fifth series, edited by Peter Laslett and James Fishkin (Yale University Press: New Haven, Connecticut, 1979), p. 239.

17. Barber, *Strong Democracy*, p. 188.

18. Pateman, *Problem of Political Obligation*, p. 18.

19. Barber, *The Conquest of Politics* (Princeton University Press: Princeton, N.J., 1988), p. 18.

20. Barber, *Strong Democracy*, p. 24.

21. Ibid., p. 189.

22. Ibid., p. 182.

23. Ibid., p. 183.

24. Ibid., p. 182.

25. Ibid., p. 184.

26. Ibid., p. 46.

27. Ibid., p. 175.

28. Ibid., p. 177.

29. Ibid., p. 192.

30. But in effect, for political talk to remain alive, there is a common understanding citizens must hold in order to secure it. I have discussed elements of this understanding in chapters 3 and 5, and I discuss other elements in chapters 7 and 8. Barber does not himself deal extensively with this dimension of political talk so much as he hopes to define political talk, as well as to state its benefits. But if that talk is to survive, it is necessary to demonstrate its foundations, and clearly a key foundation is a constitutional system that secures rights in both formal and substantive senses.

31. Pateman, *Problem of Political Obligation*, pp. 14–15.

32. Ibid., p. 17.

33. Ibid., pp. 18–19.

34. Ibid., p. 19.

35. Barber, *Strong Democracy*, pp. 281–89.

36. Sartori, *Theory of Democracy Revisited*, pp. 117–18.

37. Barber, *Strong Democracy*, pp. 267–311. This is the implication of Barber's suggestions for reforms of the liberal state, all of which presume that citizens can acquire the proper knowledge to make judgments and manifest good judgment in deciding. And of course, as argued earlier, Pateman makes the same assumption throughout, for as we have seen, she argues that citizens make the best, most enlightened judgments in participatory settings.

38. The emphasis on leadership is actually understood as a key element in Barber for securing participatory democracy, pp. 237–38.

CHAPTER 7

1. Rawls, *Theory of Justice*. Rawls's well-known principles of justice are organized into two parts. The first part, which has priority over the second, says that each person is to have an "equal right to the most extensive basic liberty compatible with a similar liberty to others" (pp. 60–61). In this way, Rawls makes as basic to liberal regimes the provision of fundamental rights and liberties, such as "political liberty (the right to vote and to be eligible for public office) together with freedom of speech and assembly; liberty of conscience and freedom of thought; freedom of the person along with the right to hold (personal) property; and freedom from arbitrary arrest and seizure as defined by the concept of the rule of law" (pp. 60–61). The second principle says that social and economic inequalities are to work to the advantage of everyone (the difference principle) while ensuring that all social positions are open to all (p. 60). The principles are used to distribute primary goods, rights and liberties, powers and opportunities, income and wealth, and self-respect (which has a "central place") in a manner that is to "everyone's advantage" (p. 62). Here, unequal distributions are acceptable only if they benefit all. Rawls's notion of justice epitomizes the conception of a liberal regime described in chapter 2 because it supports a distribution of rights and liberties to all that secures the basis for self-respect and the development of persons.

2. Rawls, *Theory of Justice*, p. 454. In a well-ordered society, "the members have a strong and normally effective desire to act as the principles of justice require."

3. Rawls, "Kantian Constructivism in Moral Theory," *Journal of Philosophy* 77:9 (September 1980), p. 518. "The aim of political philosophy . . . is to articulate and to make explicit those shared notions and principles thought to be already latent in common sense or . . . if common sense is hesitant and uncertain . . . to propose to it certain conceptions and principles congenial to its most essential convictions and historical traditions." This means that the norms of a just society already exist in the culture and that a social learning process that can teach them is of critical importance.

4. Rawls, *Theory of Justice*, p. 62.

5. Ibid., p. 523.

6. This argument is a revised argument of an earlier version of the claim I made in a previous essay that Rawls's moral psychology

provides a basis for understanding the importance of an enlarged culture to the liberal regime. See my essay entitled "The Idea of a Duty to Justice in Ideal Liberal Theory," in *Liberals on Liberalism*, ed. Alfonso Damico (Rowman and Littlefield: Totowa, N.J., 1986), pp. 95–111.

7. Rawls, *Theory of Justice*, p. 464.

8. Ibid., p. 464.

9. Ibid., p. 466.

10. Ibid., p. 466.

11. Ibid., p. 466.

12. Ibid., p. 468.

13. Ibid., p. 468.

14. Ibid., p. 468.

15. Ibid., p. 471.

16. Ibid., p. 471.

17. Ibid., pp. 469–70.

18. Ibid., p. 472.

19. Ibid., p. 527.

20. Ibid., p. 527.

21. In discussing the three psychological laws of moral psychology, Rawls says that the love developed in the family and the friendly feelings and trust developed in the associations during the morality of association lead to a sense of justice. See *Theory of Justice*, p. 491.

22. Rawls, "Justice as Fairness: Political Not Metaphysical," *Philosophy and Public Affairs* 14 (Summer 1985), p. 231.

23. Ibid., p. 231.

24. Ibid., p. 232.

25. Rawls, "Kantian Constructivism in Moral Theory," p. 525.

26. Rawls, *Theory of Justice*, p. 473.

27. Ibid., p. 474.

28. Stephen L. Esquith and Richard T. Peterson, "The Original Position as Social Practice," *Political Theory* 16:2 (May 1988).

29. Rawls, *Theory of Justice*, p. 229.

30. Ibid., p. 86.

31. Ibid., p. 226.

32. Ibid., pp. 226–27.

33. Ibid., p. 137.

34. Ibid., pp. 136–37.

35. Ibid., p. 143.

36. Ibid., p. 153.

37. Ibid., p. 139.

38. Ibid., p. 139.

39. Ibid., p. 139.

40. Ibid., p. 139.

41. Esquith and Peterson, "The Original Position," p. 308.

42. Rawls, *Theory of Justice*, p. 85.

43. Esquith and Peterson, "The Original Position," p. 310.

44. Ibid., p. 310.

45. Rawls, *Theory of Justice*, p. 87.

46. Esquith and Peterson, "The Original Position," p. 313.

47. Ibid., pp. 313–14.

48. Ibid., pp. 316–17.

49. Rawls, *Theory of Justice*, pp. 72–74.

50. Ibid., p. 75.

51. Ibid., p. 83.

52. Ibid., p. 89.

53. Ibid., p. 62.

54. Ibid., pp. 96–97; see pp. 83 and 98–99 for representative man.

55. Ibid., p. 99.

56. Ibid., p. 99–100.

57. Esquith and Peterson, "The Original Position," p. 321.

58. Rawls, *Theory of Justice*, p. 199.

59. Ibid., pp. 199–200.

60. Esquith and Peterson, 'The Original Position," p. 321.

61. Rawls, *Theory of Justice*, pp. 221–28.

CHAPTER 8

1. Michael Walzer, *Spheres of Justice: A Defense of Pluralism and Equality* (Basic Books: New York, 1983), pp. 3–4. My view of Walzer's book is influenced by my reading of Emily Gill's essay "Walzer's Complex Equality: Constraints and the Right to Be Wrong," *Polity* 20:1 (Fall 1987). Gill sees Walzer as a committed liberal "committed to the autonomy of individuals" (p. 39). Thus for Gill, Walzer does not impose an insufferable collectivist ethos on people, an ethos that would undermine individual autonomy. This permits and certainly presumes that citizens may well be able to disagree with the policies of the community and thus have the right to, from the community's eyes, be wrong. Unless this position is taken, the individual is forbidden the right to challenge authority, and then the basis in Walzer for an enlarged culture would not exist. But given that the community exists to help secure individual autonomy, it is possible to demonstrate, as I hope to do in this chapter, that there is an underlying culture that secures diversity, pluralism and freedom, and this setting is the setting of the enlarged culture. Thus I think Gill is correct to argue that Walzer's view of liberty "promotes the freedom of individuals to participate in the collective decision making of the country." This activity does not prevent citizens from questioning communal decisions and thus manifesting the right to be wrong. And the reason is that Walzer protects the individual with two principles, nondiscrimination, which guarantees equal treatment, and nonrepression which guarantees democratic rights (p. 44).

2. Walzer, *Spheres of Justice*, p. 4.

3. Ibid., p. 10.

4. Ibid., pp. 100–101.

5. Ibid., p. 312.

6. Ibid., p. xiv.

7. Ibid., pp. xiv–xv.

8. Ibid., p. 41.

9. Ibid., p. 45.

10. Ibid., p. 65.

11. Ibid., p. 84.

12. Ibid., p. 84.

13. Ibid., p. 84.

14. Ibid., p. 85.

15. Ibid., p. 90.

16. Ibid., p. 90.

17. Lyle A. Downing and Robert B. Thigpen, "Beyond Shared Understandings," *Political Theory* 14:3 (August 1986), p. 462.

18. Ibid., p. 463.

19. Ibid., p. 463.

20. Ibid., p. 463.

21. For an interesting critique of Walzer along these lines, see Susan Moeller Okin, "Justice and Gender," *Philosophy and Public Affairs* 16:1 (Winter 1987).

CHAPTER 9

1. Rawls, "The Idea of an Overlapping Consensus."

2. Ibid., pp. 19–21.

3. Sartori, *Theory of Democracy Revisited*, p. 503.

4. Ibid., p. 500.

5. Allan Bloom, *The Closing of the American Mind: How Higher Education Has Failed Democracy and Impoverished the Souls of Today's Students* (Simon and Schuster: New York, 1987). See the excellent

review of this book by Martha Nussbaum, "Undemocratic Vistas," *New York Review of Books* 34:17, 5 November 1987. She argues that Socrates was concerned to promote "careful reasoning" in the study of practical problems and to include the broadest spectrum of the democratic society (p. 20). But she says that Bloom's Socrates is for a contemplative life for the elite who engage in a "contemplative and quasi-religious" philosophy "removed from ethical and social concerns" (p. 24). Her view of Socrates comes closer to the view that I argue is the one that the Athenians should or might have argued for.

To be fair to Bloom, it must be said that he is not unaware or unadmiring of the importance of the kind of mentality that the second Socrates I describe calls for. Bloom says, for instance, that "freedom of the mind requires not only, or not even especially, the absence of legal constraints but the presence of alternative thoughts. The most successful tyranny is not the one that uses force to assure uniformity but the one that removes the awareness of other possibilities, that makes it seem inconceivable that other ways are viable, that removes the sense that there is an outside. It is not feelings of commitments that will render a man free, but thoughts, reasoned thoughts" (p. 249).

But Bloom goes on to say that "much in democracy conduces to the assault on awareness of difference" (p. 249). In fact the "deepest intellectual weakness of democracy is its lack of taste or gift for the theoretical life" (p. 252). The university must strive for theoretical truth, and it thus must "be contemptuous of public opinion because it has within it the source of autonomy - the quest for and even discovery of the truth according to nature" (p. 254). The university must secure a space for philosophy just as Socrates tried to do. For Socrates, this task meant aligning himself with the gentlemen, elite class who had the leisure time and money to support philosophy. To do so, philosophers had to practice the art of "deception" (p. 279). They had in effect to make themselves of use to the gentlemen without letting them know what they were actually doing (p. 279). In this view, Socrates is so certain that his conduct can be the source of the truth that he is willing to deceive to achieve it. This Socrates hopes to stand with other philosophers astride the society and, like Plato, determine the "nature of things," and then organize society to attain that real nature. But in this setting an enlarged culture is surely threatened, just as is the enveloping dialog of liberal society. This Socrates is not the good friend of liberalism that Bloom would have him be.

For another view, which suggests that Socrates' perfectionism is compatible with democracy, see Richard Kraut, *Socrates and the State*

(Princeton University Press: Princeton, N.J., 1984). Kraut says that Socrates is "looking for . . . core statements . . . Once he finds them, he will be able to spell out the property that all virtuous acts have in common, and that makes them all virtuous acts: each would be chosen by someone who has knowledge of those core statements" (pp. 281–83). But because Socrates doubts that human beings will ever have the knowledge to rule well, then the state will be badly governed by whoever rules it. In this case, "there would be no point in replacing a democracy with some other form of government" (p. 208).

6. See Plato's *Apology* translated by F. J. Church, in *Euthyphro, Apology, Crito* (Bobbs-Merrill: Indianapolis, 1948). For instance, Socrates seems to exonerate himself of the charges against him, including atheism, corrupting the young, and making the weaker argument appear stronger (pp. 28–33). So what is he really guilty of? This seems to be the question he really wants to address, and he says he is guilty of following the oracle of Delphi's order to determine if there was anyone wiser than Socrates (p. 25). So he went about questioning people, and this effort at searching for truth through philosophic inquiry caused Athenians to rise up against him. "From this examination, Athenians, has arisen much fierce and bitter indignation, and as a result a great many prejudices about me" (p. 27). My view here accepts the position in part of I. F. Stone in *The Trial of Socrates* (Little Brown: Boston, 1988), especially chapters 17 and 18, that Socrates should have used a free speech argument to defend himself. My point of difference with Stone is only one of degree. What if free speech for Socrates was only valid if it led to a perfectionist framework for judgment? In this view, if free speech were used to create an accommodationist framework for judgment, it is possible that it would threaten philosophy. If this argument was rejected by the Athenians, or, in other words, if they felt that free speech could only be used to secure an accommodationist discourse as the basis for democracy, then Socrates' version of free speech would be suspect to them.

7. Bruce A. Ackerman, *Social Justice in the Liberal State* (Yale University Press: New Haven, Conn., 1980), p. 11.

8. Ibid., p. 332.

9. Ibid., p. 332.

10. Ibid., p. 332.

11. Ibid., p. 345.

12. Ibid., p. 345.

13. Ibid., p. 346.

14. Ibid., p. 345.

15. Ibid., pp. 345–46.

16. Ibid., p. 346.

Selected Bibliography

Abbott, Philip. *The Shotgun Behind the Door: Liberalism and the Problem of Political Obligation.* University of Georgia Press, 1976.

_____. Review of Richard Flathman's *Political Obligation* in *Political Theory* 5 (February 1977).

_____. Review of A. John Simmons's *Moral Principles and Political Obligations* in *Political Theory* 8 (November, 1980).

Ackerman, Bruce A. *Social Justice in the Liberal State.* Yale University Press, 1980.

Arendt, Hannah. *Lectures on Kant's Political Philosophy,* ed. Ronald Beiner. University of Chicago Press, 1982.

Arneson, Richard J. "The Principle of Fairness and Free-Rider Problems." *Ethics* 92 (July 1982).

Barber, Benjamin. *Strong Democracy: Participatory Politics for a New Age.* University of California Press, 1984.

_____. *The Conquest of Politics.* Princeton University Press, 1988.

Beiner, Ronald. *Political Judgment.* University of Chicago Press, 1983.

Bellah, Robert N. *The Broken Covenant.* Seabury Press, 1975.

_____. et al. *Habits of the Heart: Individualism and Commitment in American Life.* University of California Press, 1985.

Bloom, Allan. *The Closing of the American Mind: How Higher Education Has Failed Democracy and Impoverished the Souls of Today's Students.* Simon and Schuster, 1987.

Congleton, Ann. "Two Kinds of Lawlessness: Plato's Crito." *Political Theory* 4 (November 1974).

Dagger, Richard K. "What Is Political Obligation?" *American Political Science Review* 61 (March 1977).

_____. "Rights, Boundaries, and the Bonds of Community: A Qualified Defense of Moral Parochialism." *American Political Science Review* 79 (June 1985).

Damico, Alfonso J. "Dewey and Marx: On Partisanship and the Reconstruction of Society." *American Political Science Review* 75 (September 1981).

_____. "Is the Problem with Liberalism How It Thinks?" *Polity* 16 (Summer 1984).

_____. ed. *Liberals on Liberalism.* Rowman and Littlefield, 1986.

DeLue, Steven M. "Aristotle, Kant and Rawls on Moral Motivation in Just Society." 74 *American Political Science Review* (June 1980).

_____. "Kant's Politics as an Expression of the Need for His Aesthetics." *Political Theory* 13 (August 1985).

_____. "The Idea of a Duty to Justice in Ideal Liberal Theory," in *Liberals on Liberalism,* ed. Alfonso J. Damico. Rowman and Littlefield, 1986.

Diggins, John Patrick. *The Lost Soul of American Politics: Virtue, Self-Interest, and the Foundations of Liberalism.* Basic Books, 1984.

Downing, Lyle A., and Robert B. Thigpen. "Beyond Shared Understandings." *Political Theory* 14 (August 1986).

Dworkin, Ronald. *Taking Rights Seriously.* Harvard University Press, 1977.

_____. *A Matter of Principle.* Harvard University Press, 1985.

Elshtain, Jean Bethke. "Kant, Politics and Persons: The Implication of His Moral Philosophy." *Polity* 14 (Winter 1981).

Esquith, Stephen L., and Richard T. Peterson. "The Original Position as Social Practice." *Political Theory* 16 (May 1988).

Euben, J. Peter, "Philosophy and Politics in Plato's Crito." *Political Theory* 6 (May, 1978).

Ewin, R. E., *Liberty, Community and Justice.* Rowman and Littlefield, 1987.

Fishkin, James S. *The Limits of Obligation.* Yale University Press, 1982.

Flathman, Richard E. *Political Obligation.* Atheneum, 1972.

_____. *The Practice of Political Authority: Authority and the Authoritative.* University of Chicago Press, 1980.

_____. *The Philosophy and Politics of Freedom.* University of Chicago Press, 1987.

Galston, William A. "Moral Personality and Liberal Theory." *Political Theory* 10 (November 1982).

_____. "Defending Liberalism." *American Political Science Review* 76 (September 1982).

Geise, Jack. "Liberal Political Theory: Reconciling Ideals and Practice." *Polity* 20 (Winter 1987).

Gewirth, Alan. *Reason and Morality.* University of Chicago Press, 1978.

Gill, Emily. "Property and Liberal Goals." *Journal of Politics* 45 (August 1983).

_____. "Walzer's Complex Equality: Constraints and the Right to Be Wrong." *Polity* 20 (Fall 1987).

Green, Philip. *Retrieving Democracy: In Search of Civic Equality.* Rowman and Allanheld, 1985.

Guttman, Amy. "Communitarian Critics of Liberalism." *Philosophy and Public Affairs* 14 (Summer 1985).

_____. *Democratic Education.* Princeton University Press, 1987.

Howard, Rhoda E., and Jack Donnelly. "Human Dignity, Human Rights, and Political Regimes." *American Political Science Review* 80 (September 1986).

Kallenberg, Arthur L., and Larry M. Preston. "Liberal Paradox: Self-Interest and Respect for Political Principles." *Polity* 17 (Winter 1984).

Kant, Immanuel. *The Groundwork of the Metaphysic of Morals,* ed. H. J. Paton. Harper, 1948.

_____. "Metaphysical Foundations of Morals," in *The Philosophy of Kant* ed. Carl J. Friedrich, Modern Library, 1949.

_____. *Critique of Judgement,* trans. J. H. Bernard. Hafner Press, 1951.

_____. *Critique of Practical Reason,* trans. Lewis White Beck. Bobbs-Merrill, 1956.

_____. *Religion Within the Limits of Reason Alone,* trans. Theodore M. Greene and Hoyt H. Hudson. Harper Books, 1960.

_____. "Perpetual Peace." in *Kant on History,* ed. Lewis White Beck. Bobbs-Merrill, 1963.

_____. *The Metaphysical Elements of Justice,* trans. John Ladd. Bobbs-Merrill, 1965.

_____. *Critique of Pure Reason,* trans. F. Max Muller. Anchor Books, 1966.

_____. *Kant's Political Writings,* ed. Hans Reiss. Cambridge University Press, 1970.

_____. "Metaphysical Principles of Virtue," in *Ethical Philosophy,* trans. James W. Ellington. Hackett, 1983.

Klosko, George. "Presumptive Benefit, Fairness, and Political Obligation." *Philosophy and Public Affairs* 16 (Summer 1987).

Kraut, Richard. *Socrates and the State.* Princeton University Press, 1984.

Kuflik, Arthur. "The Inalienability of Autonomy." *Philosophy and Public Affairs* 13 (Fall 1984).

Lane, Robert. "Individualism and the Market Society." In J. Roland Pennock and John W. Chapman, *Liberal Democracy, NOMOS XXV* eds., New York University Press, 1983.

_____. "Market Justice, Political Justice." *American Political Science Review* (June 1986).

Laursen, John Christian. "The Subversive Kant: The Vocabulary of 'Public' and 'Publicity'." *Political Theory* 14 (November 1986).

Locke, John. *Second Treatise on Civil Government,* ed. Thomas P. Peardon. Bobbs-Merrill, 1952.

MacIntyre, Alasdair. *After Virtue.* University of Notre Dame Press, 1981.

Mack, Eric. "Liberalism, Neutralism and Rights." In J. Roland Pennock and John W. Chapman, eds., *Religion, Morality and the Law.* New York University Press, 1988.

MacPherson, C. B. *The Political Theory of Possessive Individualism.* Oxford University Press, 1962.

Murphy, Jeffrie. "In Defense of Obligation." In J. Roland Pennock and John W. Chapman, eds., *Political and Legal Obligation.* Atherton Press, 1970.

Neal, Patrick. "Liberalism and Neutrality." *Polity* 17 (Summer 1985).

Norman, Richard. *Free and Equal.* Oxford University Press, 1987.

Nozick, Robert. *Anarchy, State, and Utopia.* Basic Books, 1974.

Nussbaum, Martha. "Undemocratic Vistas." *New York Review of Books* 34 (5 November 1987).

Okin, Susan Moeller. "Justice and Gender." *Philosophy and Public Affairs* 16 (Winter 1987).

O' Neill, Onora. "Between Consenting Adults." *Philosophy and Public Affairs* 14 (Summer 1985).

_____. "The Public Use of Reason." *Political Theory* 14 (November 1986).

Pateman, Carole. *Participation and Democratic Theory.* Cambridge University Press, 1970.

_____. *The Problems of Political Obligation: A Critical Analysis of Liberal Theory.* John Wiley, 1979.

_____. "Political Obligation and Conceptual Analysis." In Peter Laslett, W. G. Runciman, Quentin Skinner, eds., *Philosophy, Politics, and Society.* Yale University Press, 1979.

Pennock, J. Roland, and John W. Chapman, eds., *Political and Legal Obligation.* Atherton Press, 1970.

Pitkin, Hannah. "Obligation and Consent." In Peter Laslett, W. G. Runciman, Quentin Skinner, eds., *Philosophy, Politics and Society.* Barnes and Noble, 1972.

Plato. *The Republic,* trans. Francis MacDonald Cornford. Oxford University Press, 1980.

_____. *Euthyphro, Apology, Crito,* trans. F. J. Church. Bobbs-Merrill, 1948.

Preston, Larry M. "Individual and Political Freedom." *Polity* 15 (Fall 1982).

Rawls, John. *A Theory of Justice.* Harvard University Press, 1971.

_____. "Kantian Constructivism in Moral Theory." *Journal of Philosophy* 77 (September 1980).

_____. "Justice as Fairness: Political Not Metaphysical." *Philosophy and Public Affairs* 14 (Summer 1985).

_____. "The Idea of an Overlapping Consensus." *Oxford Journal of Legal Studies* 7 (Spring 1987).

Raz, Joseph. "Authority and Justification." *Philosophy and Public Affairs* 14 (Winter 1985).

_____. *The Morality of Freedom.* Clarendon Press, Oxford, England, 1986.

Riley, Patrick. "On Kant as the Most Adequate of the Social Contract Theorists." *Political Theory* 4 (November 1973).

_____. *Kant's Political Writings.* Rowman and Littlefield, 1983.

_____. "The 'elements' of Kant's Practical Philosophy: The *Groundwork* after 200 years." *Political Theory* 14 (November 1986).

Rosenblum, Nancy L. *Another Liberalism.* Harvard University Press, 1987.

Rousseau, Jean-Jacques. *On the Social Contract, Discourse on the Origin of Inequality, Discourse on Political Economy,* ed. Donald A Cress. Hackett, 1983.

Salkever, Stephen G. "Virtue, Obligation, and Politics." *American Political Science Review* 58 (March 1974).

Sandel, Michael J. *Liberalism and the Limits of Justice.* Cambridge University Press, 1982.

_____. "The Procedural Republic and the Unencumbered Self." *Political Theory* 12 (February 1984).

_____. "Democrats and Community." *New Republic* 38:14 (22 February 1988).

Sartori, Giovanni. *The Theory of Democracy Revisited.* Chatham House, 1987.

Schoolman, Morton. "The Moral Sentiments of Neoliberalism." *Political Theory* 15 (May 1987).

Senor, Thomas D. "What if There Are No Political Obligations?" *Philosophy and Public Affairs* 16 (Summer 1987).

Simmons, A. John. *Moral Principles and Political Obligations.* Princeton University Press, 1979.

_____. "The Anarchist Position: A Reply to Klosko and Senor." *Philosophy and Public Affairs* 16 (Summer 1987).

Singer, Peter. *Democracy and Disobedience.* Oxford University Press, 1974.

Smith, Adam. *The Theory of Moral Sentiments.* Liberty Classics, 1976.

Steinberger, Peter. *Logic and Politics: Hegel's Philosophy of Right.* Yale University Press, 1988.

Stone, I. F. *The Trial of Socrates.* Little, Brown, 1988.

Sullivan, William M. *Reconstructing Public Philosophy.* University of California Press, 1982.

Tussman, Joseph. *Obligation and the Body Politic.* Oxford University Press, 1960.

Thigpen, Robert B., and Lyle A. Downing. "Liberalism and the Neutrality Principle." *Political Theory* 11 (November 1983).

Walker, A. D. M. "Political Obligation and the Argument from Gratitude." *Philosophy and Public Affairs* 17 (Summer 1988).

Walzer, Michael. *Obligations: Essays on Disobedience, War, and Citizenship.* Simon and Schuster, 1970.

_____. "Philosophy and Democracy." *Political Theory* 9 (August 1981).

_____. *Spheres of Justice: A Defense of Pluralism and Equality.* Basic Books, 1983.

_____. "Liberalism and the Art of Separation." *Political Theory* 12 (August 1984).

Index

175